NAVIGATING RESEARCH FUNDING WITH CONFIDENCE

SUCCESS
IN RESEARCH

NAVIGATING RESEARCH FUNDING WITH CONFIDENCE

CAROL SPENCELY
MARCELA ACUÑA-RIVERA
PAM DENICOLO

$SAGE

Los Angeles | London | New Delhi
Singapore | Washington DC | Melbourne

SAGE

Los Angeles | London | New Delhi
Singapore | Washington DC | Melbourne

SAGE Publications Ltd
1 Oliver's Yard
55 City Road
London EC1Y 1SP

SAGE Publications Inc.
2455 Teller Road
Thousand Oaks, California 91320

SAGE Publications India Pvt Ltd
B 1/I 1 Mohan Cooperative Industrial Area
Mathura Road
New Delhi 110 044

SAGE Publications Asia-Pacific Pte Ltd
3 Church Street
#10-04 Samsung Hub
Singapore 049483

Editor: Jai Seaman
Editorial Assistant: Lauren Jacobs
Production Editor: Manmeet Kaur Tura
Copyeditor: Jill Birch
Proofreader: Clare Weaver
Marketing Manager: Susheel Gokarakonda
Cover Design: Shaun Mercier
Typeset by: C&M Digitals (P) Ltd, Chennai, India

Library of Congress Control Number: 2019944470

British Library Cataloguing in Publication data

A catalogue record for this book is available
from the British Library

ISBN 978-1-5264-6508-5
ISBN 978-1-5264-6507-8 (pbk)

Dedication

To colleagues, friends and family who make my life interesting and fun.

Dr Carol Spencely

To my husband, family and researchers who have enriched my life with their own stories.

Dr Marcela Acuña-Rivera

To all those who supported me throughout my career and have made it stimulating and enjoyable.

Professor Pam Denicolo

Contents

List of further resources

Activities

Information box

Reflection point

Voice of experience

Example

Top tips

Figures

About the authors

Carol Spencely is a Teaching Fellow in the Faculty of Engineering and Physical Sciences at the University of Surrey. She has previously led a development programme for Early Career Research staff within the Doctoral College at the University of Surrey, and was a founder of the Postdoc Development Centre at Imperial College London where she also worked as a postdoctoral researcher. Carol has created and led workshops on preparing funding proposals for research staff and for PhD students, and also set up the 'First Funding Programme' which is a support package tailored for researchers putting in their first funding application. Carol has co-authored a book entitled, *What Every Postdoc Needs to Know* and has produced booklets for both Imperial and the University of Surrey collating advice from experienced researchers on funding applications. She has extensive experience of preparing researchers for funding interviews and coaching researchers through the funding processes.

Marcela Acuña-Rivera is Research Development Manager at Royal Holloway, University of London, UK (formerly at the University of Surrey). She was previously a researcher in Environmental Psychology in her home country, Mexico, and the UK, and her work was recognised by the Risk Analysis Society (USA) and the Surrey Centre for Excellence in Professional Training and Education (SCEPTrE; UK). Currently, she combines her research skills with her experience in research funding and provides advice and support to researchers at different stages of the application process since the identification of funding opportunities to the provision of peer-review comments, including impact, open access and data management plans. She sits in internal bid evaluation committees, provides comments as a lay person and from the funder's remit. As part of her role, she also participates in strategic University committees aimed at improving research success and funding processes and organises workshops and events to encourage multidisciplinary collaboration and funding applications.

Pam Denicolo's research, and that of her doctoral students and colleague co-researchers, has been wide-ranging, covering science, psychology, professional education and health topics across the full range of educational sectors, from young children to adult/professional, and the social and developmental issues that inflict themselves upon older and disabled people. She has supervised over 60 doctoral researchers to successful completion and examined more than twice as many. In recent years her focus has returned increasingly to postgraduate and professional education and constructivist research. Having established a Graduate School at Reading and an inter-university Graduate Centre prior to her retirement, she now provides advice, consultancy and training workshops to a range of universities worldwide on doctoral research support and training, and on research methods, particularly those based in the interpretivist paradigm. She is a founder editor and writer for the *Success in Research* Sage series.

Acknowledgements

With thanks to all the researchers and colleagues who aided us in preparing this book by sharing their experience, wisdom and expert advice. Special thanks to Phil Lidiard for his help with the chapter on finance. We would like to acknowledge contributions from:

Dr Melanie Bailey, University of Surrey, UK

Dr Marianne Coleman, University of Surrey, UK

Professor Carol Lane, University of British Columbia, Vancouver, Canada

Phil Lidiard, Research Support Manager, University of Surrey, UK

Professor Monique Raats, Director of the Food, Consumer Behaviour and Health Research Centre, University of Surrey, UK

Dr Julie Reeves, University of Southampton, UK

Prologue

Who is this book for?

Conducting research is something all of us do daily, if informally, to help with decision-making; many of us conduct research in a more formal manner to add to knowledge and to inform professional decision-making. It is the latter group for whom we wrote this book in recognition that formal research, from doctorates, through postdoctoral, general academic and Fellowship levels, that is not funded directly within industrial and commercial professions, always requires some form of financial support acquired through **bids** directed towards various kinds of **funders**.

It takes some considerable skill to win such funding, not least because the world of research funding is considerably complex with somewhat bizarre and even quirky rules, many of which are tacit, not readily available to initiates. Finding out what to ask for, how to ask for it and at whom to address our pleas is fraught with tortuous channels, replete with stormy seas and tricky sandbanks so that some people spend a lifetime traversing them with little to show for it in the end. If only they had asked fellow travellers on occasion to show them a clearer route or a short-cut or the best way to trim their sails, they might have been more successful. We are concerned here to make transparent some of the rules that we have grappled with, to de-mystify some rituals and to dispel myths.

The authors are fellow travellers, each bearing some scars but also with tales of relatively secret by-ways, kind trade winds and joyful encounters, who also have some ideas about who else might provide tug boats, pilots and itineraries to aid others along the way. Enough of the metaphor! We have joined together to add to and share the literature and contacts that we have used to fund our own research and that of others.

Thus, we hope that this book will prove useful to newer researchers, indeed to those only yet contemplating a doctorate and concerned about seeking funding to support such study, as well as to those embarking on a quest to extend their research activities.

What is unique about this book?

We are well aware that there are many books available from erudite authors detailing a range of aspects within the research funding world, especially proposal writing. We have referenced several within the book as Further reading on specific topics. However, what we sought to achieve in writing this book is to provide a succinct, accessible, real-life and practical guide to research funding, looking at, and also beyond, the authoring of a proposal to include the voices of others who influence and partner the research cycle.

Thus, we include perspectives from specific funders, government and other policy-makers, industry and the public as contributors to and beneficiaries of research. Further, we examine the realm of UK and EU funding in a global context, since, though we are a multinational team of authors, our experience is primarily UK/Europe-based. However, where appropriate we have drawn comparisons, illustrations and examples from around the world, especially when making generic points.

Our own experience of conducting research is in different disciplines, spanning the sciences, social sciences and arts/humanities, so we have endeavoured to include both a variety of disciplinary perspectives and multi- or cross-disciplinary perspectives, often drawing on the Voices of Experience of colleagues from the UK and further afield.

How can you make best use of this book?

To aid navigation of this book we have divided it into three sections. The first section explores the context of research funding which influences how it operates. This allows the reader, before becoming embroiled with the minutiae of writing the many sections of a **grant** proposal, to reflect on their research area, why they want funding and how their research ambitions might fit with the global, national and local funders' strategic priorities. Becoming oriented to those priorities saves time and effort, substantially aiding the process of bidding for research funding.

The middle section of this book looks in great depth at the realities of composing a funding application. We provide practical and frank advice on managing the project of preparing an application, including timeframes, managing other people, seeking feedback during the section writing and compilation process and responding effectively to it, as well as managing your own time and responses to challenges. We discuss the content and writing of each section of a proposal, including the thorny area of finance and budgets, and suggest a range of sources of further help, some of which may be locally accessible. We also engage with some of the new jargon that has invaded the world of research, mostly bringing new adventures to our notice through such tasks as demonstrating impact, public engagement and preparing material for open access.

The final section of the book examines the steps that follow the delivery of the application to the funder. Although it may seem that you need not read that section until you reach that happy stage, we emphasise that it is important in guiding your preparation of the proposal to understand what happens to your application once it reaches the funder's hands. We provide examples and insights into the review and assessment processes, drawing on advice from funders, reviewers, panel members and previous applicants in addition to university teams who support funding applications, and then those who support the establishment of a successfully funded project. Included is advice on how to spend your time productively while awaiting the result and suggestions about decisions to be made after an offer is received. We close the book by making explicit the many preparatory activities with which you should engage when accepting the funding offered, including reflections from those who have successfully navigated through at least one channel of the funding world.

While we suggest that for everyone, but especially those new to seeking research funding, there are benefits in working their way through the three sections in the order presented, we recognise that some readers will be anxious to find out more detail about specific stages in the process and so will inevitably start their journey through the book at different points to suit their needs. To accommodate that we have provided signposts throughout the book to indicate where topics are included, perhaps in greater depth, in other chapters in this book or in our sister books in the *Success in Research* series. We have also deliberately included some redundancy, some repetition of key advice or ideas that have relevance to more than one section of a proposal or stage of research. For instance, you will discern a thread about seeking and reflecting on feedback in other chapters than the one specifically dedicated to the why and how of soliciting and using feedback. This reflects our belief and contention that research itself, and certainly seeking funding for it, should be a collaborative adventure in which the support of peers is essential.

Voice and vocabulary

Throughout this book we have endeavoured to engage you in a conversation. We have imagined you in diverse circumstances but each of you with a desire and need to bid for research funding not merely competently, but well. Therefore, we have drawn on many voices to ensure that this conversation recognises and benefits from a range of perspectives. You may find that you can identify the contributions of the different authors despite our editorial efforts to bring some consistency to the presentation. We hope that, rather than making this a disjointed flow of discourse, it makes it more accessible and enjoyable, inviting you to join in the conversation.

Reflecting the diverse and quirky world in which research takes place, there are sometimes differences in terminology and of course there is a wealth of technical jargon that might well be interpreted slightly differently according to discipline, context and even historical time. To accommodate these challenges to communication we have provided a Glossary of Terms which is not composed of dictionary definitions, rather it explains how we have used the terms in this book, our intended meanings.

Further, to aid smooth reading, we have selected some terms to use consistently throughout the book though we recognise that alternative words are used elsewhere. For example, we use the word **data** to represent the products of research rather than expanding it constantly to include the information derived from all disciplines. We have also used the term 'doctoral researcher' to encompass those people engaged in doctoral research (whatever the degree title) in any country since in some regions they are deemed to be students and in others they are junior staff.

We hope you will bear with us as you read and not find it too difficult to translate our ideas into your context, disciplinary and geographical, and into your situation, the level of experience you have as a researcher. In this increasingly complex world of research, we are all novices in some respects and depend on each other not only to share ideas and support but to bring some humour and joy into our work. Fascinating though research can be, it can always be improved by working with convivial colleagues.

We invite you now to join us in further exploration of the quirky world of research funding.

PART I
Describing the world of research

1

The context for research funding

In this chapter you will be introduced to:

- The global challenges as drivers for regional and national research funding
- Research impact
- Research culture
- Assessment of research excellence
- Open Access (OA)

Introduction

Navigating the world of research can be a highly rewarding experience but, to benefit from the range of research funding opportunities available, you need to understand its wider context. Research does not happen in isolation and funding agencies usually allocate funds based on global, regional, national, institutional or more local drivers including their own priorities. Even though global challenges may influence lower-level priorities, each region or country will also want to address their specific needs and may allocate more funds to research projects that meet their own aims.

Understanding the influence that the key drivers of research have in setting up the global or national agendas is critical because it will help you identify the topics and challenges that, for instance, your government and other funding agencies are more interested in and thus where they may direct more financial support. For example, the United Nations (UN) have recognised that poverty, food security, clean water and good health are among the most important challenges of our era and that all countries should contribute to their solution. As a result, several countries have included these challenges as part of their national funding agenda.

This chapter aims to help you to consider the wider context when planning your research and to reflect on how you can help with tackling these challenges. Different countries may seek different research outcomes and it will be important that you identify what matters to your research funder (whether national or international), your institution and your country. In doing so, you will also increase your chances of success in securing research funding.

The global challenges

Different world organisations, such as the United Nations, set their priorities based on global challenges and they urge all member countries to embrace these and work more collaboratively when implementing their national plans. One way of implementing their plans to address their strategic priorities is through the allocation of financial support aimed at funding research that helps to tackle such challenges. As a result, major national and international funding agencies are going through a period of rapid change where local and global needs influence a large proportion of their funding priorities.

One of the most influential world agreements is the *2030 Agenda for Sustainable Development*, adopted by all United Nations Member States in 2015 (Paris), which provides a framework for peace and prosperity for people and the planet, now and into the future. In their agenda, there are 17 Sustainable Development Goals (SDGs) which are an urgent call for action to tackle poverty, inequality, climate change, environmental degradation, food security, peace, justice and other global problems. To achieve this, all member countries should develop strategies that 'improve health and education, reduce inequality, and spur economic growth – all while tackling climate change and working to preserve our oceans and forests'.

In response, several countries have implemented a number of actions that contribute to the aims of this agenda, including the allocation of more funding to research areas directly associated to the 17 goals stated in the 2030 agenda. This means that, besides supporting their national priority areas, they will also provide funding to research aimed at achieving the global SDGs. Information Box 1.1 includes some examples of how these global challenges have influenced regional and national research priorities.

Information Box 1.1

Sustainable Development Goals (UN, 2015) and its impact on funders' funding priorities

Level	Funding agencies	Examples of research funding available
Global	The Global Innovation Fund (GIF)	GIF is an international economic development charity established by governments of the United States, United Kingdom, Sweden and Australia. As part of its funding areas, they are now supporting innovation projects that help achieve the ambitions set out in the Sustainable Development Goals (SDGs). GIF is also calling other funders to work collaboratively to deliver the SDGs.
Regional	European Research Council (ERC)	Horizon Europe, the new ERC framework programme for research and innovation 2021–27 and successor of Horizon 2020, will help to deliver the European Union's strategic priorities such as the implementation of the Sustainable Development Goals and the Paris Agreement on climate. One of its funding 'pillars' is aimed at tackling global challenges and promoting industrial competitiveness.
National	Australia	The Australian Centre for International Agricultural Research (ACIAR) is contributing to the Sustainable Development Goals by funding research partnerships between Australian scientists and their counterparts in developing countries.
	UK Research and Innovation (UKRI)	The UK strategy for the Global Challenges Research Fund (GCRF) contributes to realising the ambitions of the UK aid strategy and to making progress on the global effort to address the UN Sustainable Development Goals.

Another global challenge (and an opportunity for researchers) that is influencing the research agenda in many countries is that associated with *population ageing* and its implications for health and wellbeing. Although our understanding of population ageing is most advanced in developed countries, particularly in Europe and Northern America, two-thirds of the world's older persons live in developing regions and the proportion is growing fast. In 2050, older persons are expected to account for 35% of the population in Europe, 28% in Northern America, 25% in Latin America and the Caribbean, 24% in Asia, 23% in Oceania and 9% in Africa (UN, 2017).

World organisations such as the United Nations (UN) and the World Health Organization (WHO) have put plans and programmes in place to increase our understanding of the implications of an ageing population and how to help people to live better. Consequently, governments and other agencies are directing more funds to support research into these areas such as through UK Research and Innovation (UKRI), the European Research Council (ERC) (via H2020 and the forthcoming Horizon Europe programmes) and the National Institutes of Health (NIH) in the USA. The Velux Stiftung (a research foundation in Switzerland) adopted some of the priorities set up by WHO regarding healthy ageing and is directing more funds to support basic or applied research on healthy ageing in several fields such as biology, medicine, psychology and neurosciences.

The digital transformation of societies, artificial intelligence (AI) and the internet of things (IoT) are other very important research priorities of our time. Modern societies are practically surrounded by electronic systems, devices and resources that generate or process big data such as social media, mobile phones and online games. Despite the accelerated progress in these areas, more research investigating other innovative uses and potential impacts is needed. Governments, funders and industry are increasing their financial support to research that generates or uses large bodies of data in order to inform policy development and effective interventions in areas such as medicine, healthcare, climate change, energy, agriculture, education and robotics, to name a few. For example, the Social Sciences and Humanities Research Council in Canada has among its six challenge areas to explore and understand better the complexities of the digital age including its societal, environmental and economic impact. Similarly, more research investigating current and new AI applications in different areas such as medical diagnostics and remote sensing are needed.

Finally, research investigating the presence of plastics in the environment (e.g. oceans, soil and air) and the food chain (e.g. animals, plants) is growing and rapidly becoming an emerging priority. Governments and research funders from several countries are directing financial support towards zero plastic waste (UK) and other areas such as higher quality plastics, effective recycling, food packaging and micro-plastics.

The challenges and examples presented in this section are not intended to be exhaustive but to illustrate how some countries or regions have responded to global agendas in addition to their own research priorities. There are funders who, as part of their remit, have already been supporting research in these areas and their efforts will create synergy with other agencies and stakeholders who are funding research to tackle the global challenges.

We recommend that you conduct a search to identify the specific research priorities and associated funding opportunities in your own country; these are usually included in your government's delivery plan or in their research funding allocation. You can also look at national and international funders' delivery plans or strategies to find out what challenges they are interested in and the type of research they are more interested in funding. See Reflection Point 1.1 for an exercise that may help you shape these agendas as an expert in your discipline.

Reflection Point 1.1

How you can influence the research funding agenda

You can influence the national and international governmental or funding research agendas by:

- Responding to research funding or strategic consultations that are relevant to your field. In doing so, you will learn what these decision-makers are interested in and your views will help them to shape new funding programmes and opportunities. They certainly want to hear from you as an expert in the area.
- Participating as a reviewer or as a member of relevant funding committees. This will help you understand them better and to influence their priorities and requirements. Usually, funders open public calls to invite researchers and other stakeholders to take part in their Peer Review College or panels. Make the most of these opportunities and you will also increase your chances of success when seeking funding for your research.

Considering these points, reflect on what steps you could take to influence the research agenda.

Research impact

Some funders only have one criterion for assessment, which is excellent research that enhances our understanding of the world, whereas others also give weighting in their decision to the demonstrable impact that research makes to society and economic growth. This is called research impact and some funders require applicants to clearly state what the potential impact of their research will be and how they will achieve it (pathways to impact) as part of their application. Information Box 1.2 shows the three types of impact that have traditionally been recognised by research funders.

Information Box 1.2

Research impact

Type of research impact	Definition
Academic	The demonstrable contribution that your research (basic or applied) makes within and across disciplines. This may include advances in understanding, theories, methods and intervention/applications.
Social	The contribution that excellent research brings to society, wellbeing and quality of life.
Economic	The effects that your research has on the economy in a specific area or sector including changes in industry, technology, public services and jobs.

Based on the literature, we have identified some principles that are central to impact:

a. Public engagement is crucial to achieve impact. This is a two-way process where researchers and communities talk to each other to enhance research, promote learning and develop further skills.
b. You can enhance the quality of your research and generate impact by engaging with the potential beneficiaries and users of your research at the early stages of the proposal to develop it jointly. This is called co-creation of research.
c. Multidisciplinary collaboration between different sectors brings the best outcome and it also maximises the impact of your research.
d. Being aware of the wider context helps you consider more innovative approaches to your research and how it can be used by the wider community.
e. Effective knowledge exchange between researchers, potential beneficiaries, industry and the public sector is key to generating impact and innovation. This means that the outcomes of your research should be translated into clear actions or guidelines that can be applied by policy-makers, industry and other relevant stakeholders such as the government.

Being aware of the potential impact of your research is good practice and, although not all funders include a specific section in their application forms, they will want to see how your research will make a difference to society or the specific groups they target when funding research. Please see Voice of Experience 1.1 for an example of this.

Voice of Experience 1.1

Professor Monique Raats gives an example about impact in her research field

Nutrition labelling helps consumers to make informed food choices. The Food, Consumer Behaviour and Health Research Centre (FCBH) has conducted a number of studies on how people make use of and understand the labels on food products.

These studies have been used by UK and EU regulators in forming labelling policies and constructing food information regulations. FCBH research developed a typology that helps to understand the difference between different labelling systems used around the world (Hodgkins et al., 2012), grouping them according to directiveness, i.e. the extent to which the labels provide explicit advice about product healthfulness.

In May 2012 the four UK governments launched a joint food labelling consultation. One of the questions put to consultees resulted from FCBH's findings (Hodgkins et al., 2012). By October 2012, Anna Soubry (Health Minister) announced that the UK Government would work towards a consistent Front of Pack (FOP) scheme based on a hybrid approach of % Guideline Daily Amounts (GDA) and traffic light colour coding. This is in line with the findings of the FCBH research (Malam et al., 2009; Hodgkins et al., 2012). This approach gained the support of all the leading retailers in the UK, many of whom were previously resistant to harmonization. Technical guidance for implementation of the new hybrid label was issued in June 2013. This technical guidance cited FCBH research that showed that market penetration (e.g. see Storcksdieck et al., 2010) is key to consumers noticing and becoming familiar with labelling information.

Governments and industry promote nutrition labelling as a tool to help consumers make healthy, informed food choices. Voluntary provision of FOP nutrition labelling, often referred to as 'signpost' labelling, has become widespread; however, food manufacturers and retailers have introduced it in different forms and the plethora of schemes and their differing presentation on pack may cause confusion for the consumer (Malam et al., 2009). Existing FOP schemes range from the presence of a detailed label on the front of the pack communicating the nutritional content of a range of key nutrients, possibly overlaid with interpretative text or colour as a benchmark, through to the presence of a simple visual symbol or 'logo' indicating that the product is considered to be a more healthful choice.

To underpin development of UK food policy, the UK Food Standards Agency (FSA) undertook a large-scale study in 2008 to extend the evidence base. The FCBH team based at Surrey led the design (BMRB Social Research & University of Surrey, 2008) of this UK governmental programme of research. An objective assessment of how FOP labels enable shoppers to make informed decisions, including measurement of how the different elements in existing UK FOP schemes influence decision-making and comprehension was performed. Overall, the study concluded that a single hybrid FOP label including text, traffic light and % GDA would bring comprehension and behaviour in relation to healthier purchasing choices closer together.

The UK implemented the hybrid traffic light system in June 2013. Despite initial resistance major companies are now implementing the traffic light system on their products. South Korea and Ecuador have also introduced traffic light systems, whereas others such as Finland and Chile are going a step further and introducing warning labels.

Sources

BMRB Social Research & University of Surrey (2008) Comprehension and use of UK nutrition signpost labelling schemes: Scientific Rationale and Design. London: Food Standards Agency. http://webarchive.nationalarchives.gov.uk/20120206100416/http://food.gov.uk/multimedia/pdfs/quantrationale.pdf

(Continued)

Hodgkins, C., Barnett, J., Wasowicz-Kirylo, G., Stysko-Kunkowska, M., Gulcan, Y., Kustepeli, Y., Akgungor, S., Chryssochoidis, G., Fernández-Celemin, L., Storcksdieck, S., Gibbs, M. & Raats, M. (2012) Understanding how consumers categorise nutritional labels; a consumer derived typology for front-of-pack nutrition labelling. *Appetite*, 59, 806-17.

Of course, what is considered to be impactful can be influenced by both social and research cultural priorities. We now go on to explore research culture in more detail.

Research culture

Understanding the values and behaviours that the research community have at national and international levels is crucial to your research career. Even though the research culture of specific disciplines and organisations has been under-examined, all researchers behave in specific ways that comply with the norms and beliefs within their disciplines and institutions.

The concept of culture as defined in the social sciences can be used to describe what research culture means although the set of values and behaviours would be specific to the research community. The Royal Society in the UK, for example, has started a Changing expectations programme of work to explore how the UK can promote the cultural conditions that will best 'enable excellent research and researchers here and elsewhere to flourish in the future'. They define research culture as a concept that 'encompasses the behaviours, values, expectations, attitudes and norms of our research communities. It influences researchers' career paths and determines the way that research is conducted and communicated'.

Irrespective of the definition, it is clear that research culture is important because it shapes how we do research. It involves implicit or explicit rules, values, attitudes, beliefs, knowledge, language and behaviours that are shared by members of the research community. Even though these sets of values and behaviours may vary across disciplines, groups and organisations, there are some principles that demonstrate good practices and that matter to all. See Figure 1.1 for an illustration of these principles.

The Responsible Research and Innovation Framework (RRI) acknowledges that scientific research can elicit some questions, controversies and unintended adverse reactions from the public. Researchers, governments and funding bodies are urged to consider any negative perceptions that may arise from research and to address them in an open, inclusive, transparent and timely manner at the very early stages of the research process. This will minimise any negative impacts and increase public acceptability.

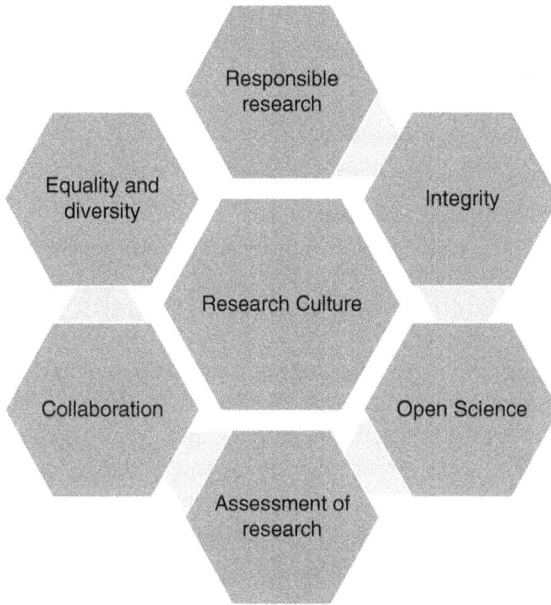

Figure 1.1 Principles of research culture

Responsible research should create spaces and use different approaches to open a frank dialogue with the public regarding the objectives and the expected outcomes of the research. This open debate goes beyond (but includes) ethical and risk considerations of the project, and the ultimate aim is to explore and effectively address any concerns and anxieties people may have on your research. The discussion may change the direction of the research and innovation process and will help advance your understanding of the research topic.

Using RRI as a framework, we recommend that you think about the likely reactions or controversies your research may produce in the public, and whether it has ethical or moral components that may elicit any concerns in the public. Asking other colleagues or relevant people is also advisable as their views will help you determine the need to explore the public's views in more detail. See Activity 1.1.

Activity 1.1

Considering ethical and moral components to your research

- List the key themes and steps in your research. Draw these out on flip-chart paper, put on post-it notes, or make a digital version using, for example, mind-mapping software.

(Continued)

- Do any of these themes or steps have an ethical dimension? If so, note it down.
- Have you considered: Equality and diversity? Public engagement? The implications of your potential findings? Open access to your data and research outputs?
- How do you know that you have covered all possibilities?
- Who can you ask for help? Note down possible people to ask. Then consider what advice you would like and distil appropriate questions based on the information exercise above.

RRI is also related to other core aspects of good research practices such as:

- **Research integrity and governance** includes policies and processes to ensure that research is conducted in a safe, honest, transparent, respectful and ethical manner. Researchers' behaviours and practices should align to the highest standards of rigour and integrity. Several countries and organisations worldwide have signed research integrity statements including Singapore (*Singapore Statement on Research Integrity*), European Science Foundation (*European Code of Conduct for Research Integrity*), and the UK (the *Concordat to Support Research Integrity*).
- **Equality, inclusion and diversity** should be integral to high-quality research. Research communities must embrace these principles and help reduce the long-standing inequalities in the research world. Everyone must have the opportunity to flourish in research regardless of their gender, age, sexuality, ethnicity, disability, social class, seniority, or other characteristics.

This emphasis on fairness and equality goes further as researchers seek to share their work with each other and the public, as we discuss next.

Open research

Today, making research outputs and data open access is at the centre of scholarly research. This movement originated in the early 1990s in response to the high publishing costs and the restrictive rules that did not allow authors to make their peer-reviewed outputs freely available online to the benefit of the wider community including: other researchers, relevant stakeholders and the public. This was even more concerning for outputs that resulted from research paid for using public funds and conducted by researchers employed by public institutions.

The debate rapidly gained more advocates and two decades later several countries and organisations have committed to the principles of open access. A number of declarations have been supported worldwide such as the *Budapest Open Access Initiative* (BOAI, 2001), the *Bethesda Statement on Open Access Publishing* and the

Berlin Declaration on Open Access to Knowledge in the Sciences and Humanities, both released in 2003. The BOAI declaration was updated in 2012 and has been signed by a vast number of countries and funding agencies around the world. New open access recommendations including not just publications but free online access to any type of scholarly research outputs such as raw data, metadata and digital outputs were developed.

Open Access (OA) means free online access to research outputs and many authors have argued that it increases readership, visibility and the number of citations although this has not been scientifically proven. Other factors such as reputation of the author(s) and the journal, discipline and international collaboration may affect the output's impact. The true value of the open access movement is that people from all over the world can have access to state-of-the-art research without paying high-cost subscriptions because this has already been paid by the funder or the researcher's institution. This is particularly beneficial to countries and researchers who cannot afford such costs.

There are two main models to make your publications open access:

- Green route or self-archiving – authors make their final accepted (peer-reviewed) manuscript open access by depositing it in an open access repository. This route has no cost and usually the publisher retains the copyright.
- Gold route – the publisher charges a cost for making the published version open access. This route uses a Creative Commons (CC) licence, which sets the terms of reuse. The author usually retains full copyright.

Since its inception in the 1990s, the OA movement has evolved considerably and today several governments and funding bodies have mandates that require researchers to not only make their publications open access but their research data too. Good practices like this make research more transparent and allow others to reuse the data in more innovative ways.

In the UK, for instance, a multi-stakeholder group involving funders and higher education universities published a Concordat on Open Research and Data (2016). This concordat outlines the key principles for ensuring that research data is 'openly discoverable, accessible, intelligible, assessable and usable in a manner consistent with relevant legal, ethical, disciplinary and regulatory framework and norms, and with due regard to the costs involved'.

The concordat sets out the expectations of best practice and defines open research data as 'those research data that can be freely accessed, used, modified, and shared, provided that there is appropriate acknowledgement if required'. Similar to other statements, the concordat recognises that 'not all research data can be open and access may need to be managed in order to maintain confidentiality, guard against unreasonable cost, protect individuals' privacy, respect consent terms, as well as managing security or other risks'.

The European Research Council (ERC) strongly supports the open access principles and in September 2018 launched the Plan S for open access to research. This plan was developed by 'cOAlition S', an international consortium of Science Europe and major national research funders from 13 European countries. Plan S requires that scholarly publications that result from research funded by participating funding bodies must be published in compliant open access journals or on compliant open access platforms. The consortium also developed 10 principles which state that, among other things, authors should retain full copyright of their publication with no restrictions and Universities, research organisations and libraries should align their policies and strategies to ensure transparency. We will not describe each principle here, but you can find them on the cOAlition S website: https://www.coalition-s.org/

The societal and economic benefits of open access have been widely recognised and supported, and it is now an acceptable and, in many cases, required route to sharing your research findings.

Another aspect of research that you should be alert to is the requirement in several countries to demonstrate the excellence of your research for your institution and to funders. We explore that next.

Assessment of research excellence

Some governments and funding agencies conduct periodical institutional assessment exercises to evaluate the quality of the research they have supported and to establish standards for future funding support. Governments may assess institutions and researchers based on different criteria such as number and quality of outputs, impact and overall research environment. Understanding the requirements and processes of these exercises will help you and your organzation consider their principles at the early stages of the research cycle.

In the UK, for example, the government uses a general framework for assessment called Research Excellence Framework (REF). According to their website at the time of writing,

> REF is conducted jointly by Research England (RE), the Scottish Funding Council (SFC), the Higher Education Funding Council for Wales (HEFCW) and the Department for the Economy, Northern Ireland (DfE). The REF is managed by the REF team, based at RE, on behalf of the four UK HE funding bodies, and is overseen by the REF Steering Group, consisting of representatives of the four funding bodies. The next REF will occur in 2021 and the primary purpose is to

produce assessment outcomes for each submission made by institutions. These outcomes deliver the wider threefold purpose of the exercise, as follows:

a. The four HE funding bodies intend to use the assessment outcomes to inform the selective allocation of their grant for research to the institutions which they fund, with effect from 2022–23.
b. The assessment provides accountability for public investment in research and produces evidence of the benefits of this investment.
c. The assessment outcomes provide benchmarking information and establish reputational yardsticks, for use within the HE sector and for public information.

The REF is a process of expert review with expert sub-panels for each of 34 units of assessment (UOAs) who will carry out the assessment, working under the leadership of four main panels. The REF is a single framework for assessment across all disciplines that usually occurs every six years. It is aimed at evaluating data from all research active staff and their number of outputs, research doctoral degrees awarded, research income, impact case studies, and the institutional research environment, all related to the period of assessment. Equity, equality and transparency govern the conduct of the REF and, even though individual researchers are required to contribute to REF, the submission is at institutional level. Results are used by the Higher Education funding bodies to inform future research funding.

The UK is also developing a new form of evaluation for the sector called Knowledge Exchange Framework (KEF). Similar to the origins of REF, this is a consultative process 'that it is intended to increase efficiency and effectiveness in use of public funding for knowledge exchange (KE), to further a culture of continuous improvement in universities by providing a package of support to keep English university knowledge exchange operating at a world class standard. It aims to address the full range of KE activities' (Research England, accessed April 2019).

Australia also conducts a research evaluation framework called *Excellence in Research for Australia (ERA)*. According to their website, the objectives of ERA are to:

- establish an evaluation framework that gives government, industry, business and the wider community assurance of the excellence of research conducted in Australian higher education institutions;
- provide a national stock-take of discipline level areas of research strength and areas where there is opportunity for development in Australian higher education institutions;
- identify excellence across the full spectrum of research performance;
- identify emerging research areas and opportunities for further development;
- allow for comparisons of research in Australia, nationally and internationally, for all discipline areas.

ERA evaluates performance within each discipline at each university and gives us a detailed view of the research landscape in Australia, from quantum physics to literature. It highlights national research strengths in areas of critical economic and social importance across all disciplines. In addition, ERA results highlight the research strengths of individual universities. The ERA data presented in each National Report also provides contextual information about research application, knowledge exchange and collaboration.

Overall, researchers, institutions and governments should all work together to create an innovative research community that pursues high-quality research and embraces good research practices. Talk to your colleagues about your ideas and values, and together you can help to inspire and shape a good environment that generates and celebrates high-quality research.

Further reading

The Budapest Declaration (2001) for open access. Available at: https://www.budapestopenaccessinitiative.org/read

Concordat on Open Research and Data (2016) HEFCE, Research Councils UK, Universities UK, Wellcome Trust. Available at: https://www.ukri.org/files/legacy/documents/concordatonopenresearchdata-pdf/ (Accessed: April 2019)

Excellence with Impact (UKRI). More details at: https://www.ukri.org/innovation/excellence-with-impact/ (Accessed April 2019)

Excellence in Research for Australia (ERA). Please see the website for further information: https://www.arc.gov.au/excellence-research-australia (Accessed April 2019)

Harnad, Stevan (2015) Open access: what, where, when, how and why. In J. Britt Holbrook and Carl Mitcham (Eds), *Ethics, Science, Technology, and Engineering: An International Resource* (2nd edition of *Encyclopedia of Science, Technology, and Ethics*), Farmington Hills MI: Macmillan. Available at: https://eprints.soton.ac.uk/361704/1/ESTEarticle-OA-Harnad.pdf (Accessed April 2019)

Knowledge Exchange Framework (KEF). Find more information on Research England's webpages: https://re.ukri.org/knowledge-exchange/knowledge-exchange-framework/ (Accessed April 2019)

Malam, S., Clegg, S., Kirwan, S., McGinigal, S., Raats, MM., Shepherd, R., Barnett, J., Senior, V., Hodgkins, C. (2009) *Comprehension and use of UK nutrition signpost labelling schemes*. Food Standards Agency, London.

Research Excellence Framework (REF). More details can be found here: https://www.ref.ac.uk/ (Accessed April 2019)

Responsible Research and Innovation Framework (RRI). More can be found here: https://www.rri-tools.eu/about-rri (Accessed April 2019)

Royal Society. Details about the Changing Expectations programme of work can be found on their webpages: https://royalsociety.org/topics-policy/projects/research-culture/ (Accessed March 2019).

Storcksdieck Genannt Bonsmann, S., Fernández Celemín, L., Larrañaga, A., Egger, S., Wills, J. M., Hodgkins, C., Raats, M. M. (2010) Penetration of nutrition information on food labels across the EU-27 plus Turkey. *European Journal of Clinical Nutrition*, 64(12): 1379–85.

United Nations (2017) World Population Ageing Report: Highlights. Department of Economic and Social Affairs. ISBN 9789211515510 Retrieved on 02 August 2019 https://www.un.org/en/development/desa/population/publications/pdf/ageing/WPA2017_Highlights.pdf

United Nations. 2030 Agenda for Sustainable Development, adopted by all United Nations Member States in 2015 (Paris), and the 17 Sustainable Development Goals (SDGs). Offical papers and further information can be found here: https://www.un.org/sustainabledevelopment/development-agenda/ (Accessed April 2019)

2

Research funders: who you could choose and why?

In this chapter you will be encouraged to consider:

- Types of research funders
- Types of research funding
- What research funders want
- Your approach to research funding
- Choosing the right funder

Introduction

Historically, scientific research has been funded using a number of sources ranging from single private sponsors to corporate, charitable and governmental funds. In modern times, we call them Research Funders and although they are all influenced by the key drivers of research as discussed in the previous chapter, research funders also have their own remit so their funding will be oriented to respond to their identified priorities based on their stakeholders' motivations and interests. Having a holistic view of the research landscape (Chapter 1), getting to know the range of funders in your research area (and beyond), and choosing the right one for you is critical for a successful **grant** application.

In this chapter we focus on the main three types of research funders that you will find when seeking to finance your research: public, private and not-for-profit organisations. We, of course, cannot cover every possible funder but instead describe some of the most representative funders in the UK and other countries. This will provide a framework, thus making you better equipped to choose the right funder for your research. You certainly will be able to find other funders when conducting a more focused and in-depth search, but we hope that this chapter helps you better understand funders and the world of research funding.

Types of research funders

Researchers at all levels of seniority frequently ask themselves, or their colleagues, who might financially support their research. This is not a trivial question. Understanding the types of research funders and their remit is important when deciding where to submit an application. It will help you to increase your probability of success.

Overall, there are three types of external research funders and although their priority areas may look similar, their funding sources and expected outcomes tend to differ: Government (public funds), Charities (philanthropic/public funds) and Industry/corporate organisations (private funds). The first two are defined as not-for-profit funders because they seek to advance human knowledge and increase our understanding with the goal of creating social and economic impact, rather than to earn profit for owners. However, that does not mean that they fund anything that advances knowledge because they have other motivations and interests than simply profit, as we shall see in their general agendas later in this chapter. Since they are essentially using public funds and have the same motives, most research funding from inside universities are a subset of government funding, though they may sometimes draw their finance from either charitable endowments or industrial sources. Industry, on the other hand, is business driven and they fund research to both tackle societal challenges and to generate evidence-based knowledge that fulfils their own needs. There are usually both tax and advertising advantages to such organisations of providing financial and other resources to researchers. Such profit motives are not to be disparaged because their support to the research community is largely a win-win situation. The only proviso is that they are likely to be more restricted in the kinds of research they fund and may require specific contracts that limit or specify what can be published and where.

Most of the research funders award grants through competitive processes that help them select the best research proposal for their strategic priorities and needs; therefore, it is worth spending time in finding as much information as possible about them to become familiar with their priorities, funding schemes, eligibility and assessment criteria. The next section discusses in more detail the types of funders, what they fund and how to select the best funder for you.

Government funding

Governments worldwide are interested in supporting research that helps them make decisions and tackle current and future socio-economic challenges. Thus, each country allocates funds in accordance with their strategic plans and policies and puts processes in place to deliver their research agenda.

Most countries have a designated research council or councils related to specific discipline areas to fund research. However, there could be other national institutions that provide direct funding such as the Ministry of Defence, Environmental Agencies, National Research Institutes, Department of Energy, and so on.

As an example, UK Research and Innovation (UKRI) is an important funder in the UK government and it is sponsored by the Department for Business, Energy and Industrial Strategy (BEIS). Its 'main purpose is to invest in and facilitate research and innovation activities across the United Kingdom, and, through Research England, directly support higher education providers in England to carry out research and knowledge exchange activities' (p6, UKRI, 2018).

UKRI funds excellent research that promotes innovation as well as societal and economic impact. It seeks to connect researchers and innovators with customers, users and the public in order to maximise the benefit and impact of the research they fund. It comprises: 1) seven councils which are organised by discipline ranging from the arts, humanities and economics to medical, biological, engineering, social sciences and physics; 2) Innovate UK (business-led innovation); and 3) Research England, which creates the conditions for a successful research exchange between UK Universities.

Another great example of a governmental initiative to fund research is the European Research Council (ERC), which is funded by the European Commission and its member countries. ERC is one of the most prominent research-funding organisations worldwide. It seeks to encourage scientific excellence and frontier research necessary to meet European and global challenges such as climate change, poverty, cancer, ageing and many others. The ERC fosters collaboration across its member countries and supports research and innovation activities through several funding opportunities. Researchers from anywhere in the world can apply for ERC grants provided the research they undertake is carried out in an EU Member State or associated country.

Horizon 2020 (H2020 and its successor Horizon Programme) is the largest EU Research and Innovation programme ever, running from 2014 to 2020. It promotes collaboration between the public and private sectors to work together in delivering world-class science and innovation, industrial leadership and tackling societal challenges. It seeks to strengthen Europe's research base by supporting cutting edge and fundamental research, stimulating innovative technologies and promoting career development. H2020 is open to everyone but we recommend that you carefully read their guidelines and verify the eligibility criteria before applying to any of the ERC and H2020 funding schemes, specifically checking such things as who can be your partners or whom you must partner.

For instance, in addition to the European funding, the Nordic countries have a platform for joint research and infrastructure called Nordforsk. This is an organisation funded by the Nordic Council of Ministers including Denmark, Finland, Iceland, Norway, Sweden as well as the Faroe Islands, Greenland and the Aland Islands. To be eligible for funding, projects must normally involve participants from at least three of these Nordic countries. Its aim is to promote collaboration between these countries to strengthen them in many areas including research. Nordforsk runs several themed and open **calls** in diverse topics such as education, gender, migration, energy, health and welfare, neutron research, societal security, smart cities and urban development, Russian cooperation and arctic research.

A large number of countries worldwide have their own research councils and in Information Box 2.1 you will find a list with some examples. This does not intend to be exhaustive but to illustrate the level of existing support for research worldwide.

Information Box 2.1

Governmental funders worldwide

Country	Governmental Funder
Argentina	CONICET
Australia	Australian Research Council
	Australian Academy of Technical Sciences and Engineering
Brazil	Sao Paulo Research Foundation (FAPESP)
	National Council for Scientific and Technological Development
	The Brazilian National Council for the States Funding Agencies (CONFAP)
Canada	Canadian Institutes of Health Research (CIHR)
China	Ministry of Science and Technology of China (MOST)
	Ministry of Health of China
	National Natural Science Foundation of China (NSFC)

(Continued)

Country	Governmental Funder
Denmark	Danish Council for Strategic Research
	Danish Council for Independent Research
European Union	ERC
	Directorate-General for Regional and Urban Policy
	H2020
Finland	Finnish Government
	Finnish National Agency for Education
France	Centre National de la Recherche Scientifique (CNRS)
Germany	German Research Foundation (DFG)
Guatemala	CONCYT
India	Indian Department of Science and Technology (DST)
Ireland	Science Foundation Ireland
	Royal Irish Academy
	Environmental Protection Agency Ireland
Luxembourg	Luxembourg National Research Fund
Mexico	Consejo Nacional de Ciencia y Tecnología (CONACYT)
Netherlands	Netherlands Organisation for Scientific Research (NWO)
	Royal Netherlands Academy of Arts and Sciences (KNAW)
	Netherlands Institute for Advanced Study in the Humanities and Social Sciences
New Zealand	Health Research Council of New Zealand
	Royal Society of New Zealand
Nordic Countries	Nordforsk
Norway	The Research Council of Norway
	Norwegian Agency for Development Cooperation (Norad)
	Norwegian Academy of Science and Letters
Peru	CONCYTEC
Scotland	Scottish Government
	Royal Society of Edinburgh
Spain	Instituto de Salud Carlos III (ISCIII)
	Princess of Asturias Foundation
South Africa	Academy of Science of South Africa
	South African Medical Research Council
Sweden	Royal Swedish Academy of Sciences
	Swedish Research Council for Health, Working Life and Welfare
	Swedish Foundation for Strategic Environmental Research

Country	Governmental Funder
Switzerland	Swiss National Science Foundation (SNSF)
	Swiss Federal Institute of Technology Zurich
UK	UK Research and Innovation (UKRI)
	Department of Health and Social Care including NIHR
USA	National Institutes of Health
	The National Science Foundation

Charitable Trusts

Charitable Trusts or Foundations are independent and not-for-profit organisations that are usually funded by endowments, donations and, in a few cases, by contributions from the public sector. They follow their own interests and, among other purposes, they may conduct and/or fund high-quality research that helps them fulfil/support their own causes.

Some charities focus on specific sectors of the population or certain types of countries; others may be more interested in specific social, health or environmental problems. Their levels of funding vary in size, area of work and application processes and some can fund individuals, community groups, other charities, or research institutions including universities. Their level of funding ranges from financially small levels of funding for travel or conference attendance, through start-up funds, full project grants, to extensive funding for capital or long-term sequential projects.

The Wellcome Trust, for example, is one of the largest charitable foundations in the UK dedicated to supporting excellent science and **translational research** anywhere in the world. They support individuals, teams, resources and major initiatives in several priority areas: population health, biomedical science, humanities, social sciences, public engagement and creative industries. Wellcome has very clear application processes, terms and conditions to award their grants while their funding schemes range from small grants, standard and themed research grants to studentships, fellowships, collaborative and public engagement grants.

Information Box 2.2 provides you with some examples of large Charitable Trusts in a few countries, but remember that there are thousands of Trusts that support research in the world and in a range of disciplines and topics. If you do not know where to start, we recommend you search on the internet for national and international associations of Charitable Trusts and Foundations. Make sure you include your topic of research to narrow down the number of results. A good starting point could be the Charity Commission web-site, Funder Finder (UK only), Foundation Directory Online (USA), and the Directory of Social Change (DSC), which has a couple of publications like *The Directory of Grant Making Trusts* and *The Guide to Major Trusts*, which are hard copy publications. You can also ask your research office at your Institution (or equivalent) whether they subscribe to any research funding tools that you can use to run your own funding searches including all types of funders.

Information Box 2.2

Examples of large size Charitable Trusts supporting research

Charitable Trust	Country	Priorities
Hospitals Contribution Fund (HCF) Research Foundation	Australia	Health systems: improve the quality, efficiency, access to and equity of provision of health services
Lundbeck Foundation	Denmark	Biomedical sciences
Volkswagen Foundation	Germany	Engineering, humanities, social sciences, life sciences, natural sciences
Laerdal Foundation	Norway	Acute medicine
Jacobs Foundation	Switzerland	Education, learning, children, young people
Velux Foundation	Switzerland	Effects of daylight on humans and nature, healthy ageing and ophthalmology
Leverhulme Trust	UK	All disciplines: arts, humanities, sciences and social sciences
Wolfson Foundation	UK	Science and medicine, mental health, health & disability, education and the arts & humanities
Nesta Foundation	UK	Health, education, the creative economy and arts and culture, government innovation, innovation policy, emerging technologies
Bill and Melinda Gates	USA	Global health, global development and growth; inequality, education, vulnerable children; science and technology

---

Funding from industry

Industry or corporate funding often aims to transfer what researchers know (including skills and methods) to businesses in order to meet major industrial and societal challenges and enhance economic growth. This is called *Knowledge Transfer* and, although businesses themselves fund research to address their own needs, the significance of translational research is growing worldwide and other funders like Research Councils may fund collaborations between researchers and industry to address specific priority areas. The Industrial Strategy Challenge Fund (ISCF) in the UK is a good example of how a government brings together excellent research and business ambitions to drive innovation and create opportunities for different sectors including industry. (See Voice of Experience 2.1 for a Canadian perspective.) This type of funding is very important to researchers too because they can use their knowledge in a different manner and generate more innovative solutions to a variety of national and international challenges.

Funding approaches and mechanisms vary across regions and types of funders, and industry and corporations are not exceptions. Industrial sponsors of research may allocate funds through direct competitive processes but often they commission research to a single supplier (an individual or research group) who has the right expertise and is the best option for their project. The process that industry follows to allocate funds depends on the timescale, their budget and their needs.

Voice of Experience 2.1

Canadian research funding from industrial partners

Due to Canada's relatively small population and limited research council funding, industrial research is sought in almost every health indication most often partnering in the faculties of medicine and engineering. Industry funding is often combined with funding from governments including national and international research councils, charities, multinational corporations, small public and private companies. Multi-site research sponsored by industry is becoming more common and often includes American sites. This is because American and Canadian medical device, pharmaceutical and engineering research authorities have agreements in place and, although are separate, many researchers produce their submission dossiers to both agencies.

The government of Canada has many incubator-like companies. One of the largest is MITACS which promotes PhD, Master's and postdoctoral partnerships with industry. MITACS links both national and international students with Canadian and international schools and sponsors. Research funding for postdocs is strongly supported by industry, as the council funding is very limited. PhD studentships and Master's studentships are funded directly to the student and only via a principal investigator grant when very large.

Canadian pharmaceutical and engineering companies are often subsidiaries of large multinationals. This restricts their budget authorization for contributions to research. Large amounts (usually over 25K GBP) will need to be authorized by a head office often in the US or Western Europe. This is especially true for capital equipment and operating grant money. Due to these restrictions, direct Canadian industry funding is for smaller aspects of research including studentships, postdocs, consulting work and partnerships.

(Continued)

Independent Canadian companies who provide funding for research to academia do exist, many are biotechs, startups and biopharma. There are numerous university spin-offs in biomedical engineering pharmaceutical and analytic labs. Most are private, however, following proof of concept studies require partnership. Success often means an IPO (initial public offering) and many others move to the US for tax reasons or to float their companies on an American stock exchange.

There are, though, other sources of financial support and support in kind available for researchers beyond the major three groups and we have selected a few exemplars in the next section to guide your explorations.

Other types of research funders

Learned societies, academies or scholarly societies are non-profit professional organisations aimed at promoting the development of knowledge and progress in the field by offering memberships, career development, organising conferences, networking, publishing journals and funding research. They obtain their funding from a variety of sources including the government, foundations, individual donors and legacies and represent an invaluable source of funding for researchers at every career stage from PhD studentships, travel, conference and training grants, to research grants, prizes and fellowships. Many learned societies have great reputations and their governing bodies or councils are highly regarded as they bring together eminent researchers who, as a group, promote excellence in research, collaboration and knowledge development for the benefit of that society. For example, in the UK the Society for Research into Higher Education provides competitive funding annually in the form of 'Scoping Awards' for newer researchers to develop their research proposals and financing for larger projects focussed specifically on issues in Higher Education.

Crowdfunding for scientific research is another funding opportunity that is becoming more popular among researchers. Put simply, crowdfunding seeks to raise money from a wide number of sources and stakeholders (e.g. general public, private businesses) to fund scientific research. People 'donate' money because they believe in research and the institution carrying it out, or because they are interested in the specific research topic. Some UK universities and charitable trusts have started to use crowdfunding to raise small amounts of money to fund their research. Crowdfunding for research is growing worldwide and it could be a useful option to fund your research although there is yet a lack of a common framework and regulation that brings together the rights and responsibilities of all parties involved: donors, recipients and service providers. Therefore, we recommend that you consider the benefits and risks of this type of funding and find out what your institution's policies in this regard are, what online platforms could be useful to your research, how much this will cost and whether there are other ways of funding your research.

As a general rule though, you should always find out as much information as possible about your potential funders, no matter what their nature. The majority of them will have websites where they provide more detailed information on who they are, their funding schemes and processes to submit an application. Some of them may include examples of funded research, which is very useful in clarifying the types of research they fund. The more clarity you have on their criteria, the more you will be able to select the right funder for you. We suggest that you engage with Activity 2.1 to begin to collect such useful information for yourself.

Activity 2.1

Finding out about research funders in your discipline

This section has provided you with a quick overview and a few examples of research funders from different countries, but you can ask your research office, other colleagues and also search on the internet to find out who your main funders are likely to be and the specific areas they generally support. Begin a file of this information for future reference, including information on the following points below:

- Funder's remit and priorities
- Type of funder and schemes they support
- Eligibility and assessment criteria
- Research skills and career stage required
- Size and duration of the grant
- Closing date and application process
- Any regularly occurring funding opportunities

Having considered what general types of funders exist we now turn to consider the different kinds of research activities each might be interested in funding.

Types of research funding

The previous section presented the different types of research funders you may find when seeking funding for your research. There are, however, a number of schemes you can apply to and although funders may use different names, all of them seem to have similarities regarding options offered. Some opportunities seek to support career development or consolidation (e.g. PhD studentships, research fellowships), whereas other schemes provide funding to support research projects either dealing with specific topics or allowing for a choice of own topic within a specific discipline or research area that is within the remit of the funder (themed or managed mode and responsive mode calls respectively). Both types of proposals will be judged against the general criteria used by the funder but those responding to a theme or managed mode call will have further specific criteria to fulfil. In this section, we do not intend to be exhaustive but to describe some of the most common types of research funding; it is likely, however, that you will find other schemes when conducting a more targeted funding search.

Research training grants: PhD studentships

If you are planning to pursue a career in research, then the most popular option is to register to become a postgraduate researcher (PGR) or a doctoral researcher. There are two broad ways to fund your doctorate: one is to find a scholarship linked to a specific research project which involves working with an identified research group; and the second is to apply to an open call from a variety of funders. There are many forms of postgraduate research studies such as: Master of Philosophy (MPhil), Doctor of Business Administration (DBA), Doctor of Education (EdD), Doctor of Architecture (DArch), co-funded PhDs with industry and many other types of doctorates and research degrees, many of them linked to specific professions. There are several resources out there to help you choose the right programme for you (see another book in the *Success in Research* series for more guidance on this: *Success in Research: Fulfilling the potential of your doctoral experience*).

Similar to other types of funding, national or international PhD studentships may be available from universities, governmental bodies, private funders such as employers and charitable trusts. Each funder has its own processes and mechanisms to apply for this type of funding, but typically doctoral studentships will provide tuition fees and stipends. It is worth, however, finding out what the funder is offering because some of them may only contribute towards some costs and the applicant is expected to find funds from other sources to pay for other costs.

If you are intending to apply for doctoral funding, we recommend that you investigate further postgraduate opportunities and funding available in your discipline both at national and international level. Take your time, think what type of postgraduate studies you are looking for, contact potential research organisations (including universities) to find out more about their programmes and their research **environment**. It is always good to contact a potential supervisor to discuss your research interests and the best options for you. You can find their names under discipline lists on their websites. They may have an institutional website that describes their research interests and/or you could find out more about them and their interests and expertise on websites such as LinkedIn and Research Gate.

Research funders in some countries may also offer *Policy Internships schemes* whereby doctoral students acquire a different set of skills by working with partner organisations on a variety of relevant policy topics. Internships are available with several government and non-governmental bodies, including learned societies and organisations. The student is expected to support their work and conduct a number of activities relevant to the ethos of the organisation. This type of experience helps researchers understand governmental priorities better and will also prepare them for their future research work. We recommend you seek out and make the most of this type of opportunity, if your circumstances allow it.

If you already possess a doctorate, then you may be interested in putting your research skills to further use and expanding them. There are opportunities to do that as we describe in the next section.

New investigator grants and research fellowships

This type of funding is aimed at developing or consolidating the researcher's career. Three broad research fellowships can be identified:

Early career research fellowships are designed to help postdoctoral researchers (on completion of their doctoral studies) with the development of a more independent research career and to consolidate their research area and skills. Research fellows may act as independent investigators or be under the supervision of a more senior investigator; the research topic may be chosen by the researcher or provided by a supervisor and/or the funder. Research fellowships which promote research independence are prestigious and can enhance the reputation of the researcher.

Traditionally, fellowships can be short- or mid-term programmes where researchers conduct a piece of research, write new bids and publications, perhaps develop and extend their own network and provide the first steps towards the establishment of their research group. Early-career researchers who do not yet hold a leadership and/or permanent position within their organisation may apply. Applicants must have a doctorate or are expected to receive their award before the fellowship commences. We recommend that you check the eligibility criteria for each funder as there may be subtle differences that may be significant to you between each one of them. If successful, fellows will receive a monthly stipend, office space and organisational help.

Although **new investigator grants** are aimed at early-career researchers, they are different to research fellowships. These grants support researchers who are ready to take the next step towards their independence and become independent **principal investigators**. Different to fellowships, new investigators are expected to combine their time with a portfolio of other activities, such as other research grants or clinical duties, teaching, or administrative tasks. Applicants are expected to have already a permanent position in a **research organisation**, but eligibility criteria may vary between funders.

Mid and senior career research fellowships are aimed at freeing up time from teaching and/or administrative activities to be able to conduct a piece of research. However, these fellowships require the applicant to be independent researchers and have a track record of nationally or internationally competitive research. They must be managing their own research group and may be on their way to becoming a recognised researcher in their field.

The next section delves into the diverse world of grants to guide you in your choice of target for your proposals.

Grants

Responsive or standard grants support research projects, infrastructure projects and methodological developments aimed at helping researchers to take forward their research interests with the potential to generate significant knowledge and impact. Even though the call may be open to any research area, the proposal should align with the funder's remit.

Strategic or topic grants refer to funding opportunities that focus on a defined topic area that is of prime importance to the funder. Usually, these types of grants address complex science questions aimed at tackling major global challenges that are within the funder's remit.

Seed funding and pump-prime funds help researchers develop new and novel ideas that have potential to be further developed in larger grants. For instance, these types of grants are useful to conduct smaller research projects to test new ideas or methods, or to generate preliminary data useful to increase the competitiveness of future research grant applications. The outcomes of these types of funds also have the potential to attract more external funding.

Research centres and hubs grants

These kinds of grants enable a team to develop a centre/hub focusing on a specific topic defined either by the funder or the researchers. This scheme supports interdisciplinary research, collaboration and teamwork involving several departments/institutions. It enables universities or a research (multidisciplinary) consortium to conduct outstanding research that may consolidate or transform our understanding of a significant research topic or area. Individuals or research institutions may apply and centres are strongly encouraged to collaborate with other centres across and outside their organisations.

Networking and collaboration grants

This type of funding aims to bring together researchers, institutions, stakeholders and other relevant groups from different disciplines/sectors to develop interdisciplinary collaborations through a number of research and training activities. Networks and partnerships are expected to lead to new collaborative multidisciplinary research proposals. The British Academy is one organisation that has multiple funding schemes that encourages collaborative grants; for example, the Newton Fund has international partners in Brazil, China, Mexico, South Africa, Turkey and Vietnam. Other examples include the EU-CHINA Research and Innovation Partnership Programme (ERCIP), which supported EU researchers from universities and industry to work in China, and the Finnish Center for International Mobility, which has an Asia Programme designed to enhance collaboration on education-based research between Finland and Asia.

See the Euraxess webpages for further examples: https://euraxess.ec.europa.eu/

Public engagement and impact grants

These enable researchers to engage the public with their research. The aim is to empower the public both by making research more people-centred and by helping people in the general public to think about and use research in their daily lives. This is an increasing area of interest as governments seek to provide evidence for their use of public money.

Capital grants

Research funders support individuals or institutions to replace premises or infrastructure and improve research space utilisation. Through this, funders expect to enhance collaboration and the use of research equipment and facilities. The ultimate aim is to foster world-leading research capabilities. The kind of things that have recently received such funding are the refurbishing of buildings to provide dedicated Graduate Schools or Doctoral Colleges or laboratories for cross-disciplinary health-related research.

Travel and conference grants

Some funders support researchers to attend or organise research conferences on topics that fall within their remit. They may also provide funding to attend meetings or workshops with a research purpose. These can be useful supplements for instance for doctoral researchers with restricted funding to attend an international conference or for special interest groups within a focussed research network to share latest research practice.

Institutional grants

Universities or research organisations have research grants, fellowships and pump-priming funds to support research that will raise their research profile. These funds may come from their annual budget allocation or from external funders obtained through competitive process or donations from private funders such as alumni. As with other types of funding, look for and become familiar with their guidelines and application process.

Regardless of their financial source, research funders aim to support excellent, innovative and multidisciplinary research that helps them tackle societal and economic challenges. Each funder will have their specific purpose and your success will partly depend on how well you address their aims and requirements. See Top Tip 2.1 for further details and see Top Tip 2.2 for how to choose the right funder.

Top Tip 2.1

What research funders want

The list below includes essential criteria you would need to demonstrate when applying for research funding.

- Your research proposal should be:
  - excellent science;
  - creative and innovative;
  - ambitious and feasible;
  - impactful research;
  - value for money.

- Yours and your research team's track record must demonstrate:
  - research areas and skills;
  - responsible research and integrity;
  - previous research grants;
  - research outputs;
  - multidisciplinary teamwork, including other stakeholders/the public;
  - achievements and career recognition.

- The research environment of the host institution should:
  - be willing to host the research;
  - have the appropriate resources and infrastructure to do so;
  - provide development opportunities including mentorship, professional development training options, and collaborative support.

Spend time reading the funders' guidelines and **evaluation** criteria because these will tell you what the funder is expecting to see in your application. You can seek advice from the funder if the guidelines are not clear or ask colleagues who have had experience with that specific funder in the past; some of them may even be part of review panels and can provide good advice. Remember that you will have to find the best fit between your research and the aims of the funder to increase your chances of success; most funders will not allow you to resubmit your application if you have not achieved this or followed their guidance.

Top Tip 2.2

How to choose the right funder

Identifying potential funders that might be a good fit for your research is not a trivial matter. There are no quick steps to finding the right funder and we suggest you consider these points when choosing the next funder for your research:

- Clarify for yourself what your motivation for identifying funders is. For instance, is it for your own personal development alone or, instead, to conduct research as the principal investigator and within a team? Answers to these questions will help you determine the type of funding you should focus on when doing a search.
- Allow plenty of time for researching funders and then making applications because things may take longer than you expect.

(Continued)

- Be strategic and develop a plan to identify potential funders in your discipline. Do not approach this task in a haphazardous manner; instead use available research tools to conduct more targeted and careful searches. Use keywords, phrases and filters to organise and narrow down your search within categories such as type of funding, size and duration of the grant, country and starting date of the grant.
- Speak with other colleagues who may know more about main funders in your research area. We also recommend you look beyond the usual funders to find more opportunities, perhaps considering the possibilities of combining resources from different sources.
- Once you have identified potential funders, create a list of those that fit your career stage, discipline and needs. Review their guidelines, priorities, funding cycles, eligibility criteria and deadlines. Look for past funded projects and grantees in that specific scheme to know the type of research and researchers they have funded. You can contact the funder directly to find out more about their funding, understand their aims better and develop an ongoing relationship with them.

Research ideas that fit a funder or funders that fit your research ideas?

You may have heard that research funding is very competitive and scarce. This is a reality and researchers are required to be more creative and innovative when applying for research funding. When looking for opportunities we recommend that you look at these with an open mind and from two perspectives at least, seeking either or both of: a) funding that matches your interests and discipline; and, b) funding that might not be a perfect match for your own specific research but where you can contribute in collaboration with other researchers you know. This will expand the number of opportunities you can apply to and will also help you to work with multidisciplinary teams.

Conclusion

In conclusion, choosing a funder for your research is not straightforward and requires at least an appreciation of (if not full understanding of) the broader societal, political and economic issues that influence research funding and the funders. Having described the world of research in Part I of this book, we will move on in the next chapters to consider putting together your application, bearing in mind the caveats we have raised here about goodness of fit in a competitive environment.

Further reading

Department for Business, Energy and Industrial Strategy. UKRI Framework document (2018) Available at: https://www.ukri.org/files/about/ukri-framework-document-2018-pdf/

McLean, R. K. D., Graham, I. D., Tetroe, J. M. and Volmikn, J. A. (2018) Translating research into action: an international study of the role of research funders. *Health Research Policy and Systems*, 16: 44. Published online 2018 May 24. doi: 10.1186/s12961-018-0316-y

Social Research Association (2002) *Commissioning Social Research Good Practice Guide* (2nd edition). Available at: http://the-sra.org.uk/wp-content/uploads/Commissioning-Social-Research-good-practice-guide1.pdf (Accessed April 2019)

PART II

Putting together your application

3

Planning and managing your application

In this chapter you will be introduced to ideas for:

- Groundwork ahead of the application preparation
- Devising a schedule for preparing your application
- Sticking to the plan
- Stages post-submission

Introduction

Once you have decided where to submit a funding application you will then need to compile it. More information about the stages in the process will be covered in Chapter 4, and we will discuss in more detail the writing and content of each of the sections in Chapter 5. Here we will concentrate on coordinating the application process in a timely manner.

Groundwork ahead of the application preparation: what you will need to have already considered and accomplished

Your track record as a researcher is an important consideration in funding decisions. The funding body will want to know that the money they are investing is in safe hands. This track record is not something that you can conjure up overnight, so you will need to build this up over a number of years. So, what are funders looking for within the track record of a researcher? In essence, this usually means they will be reviewing your Curriculum Vitae (CV) to seek evidence of the ability to conduct research and communicate it to relevant people. Here are some of the things that your CV could show:

- *Evidence of having been funded previously.* The best evidence that shows you are capable of being a Principal Investigator (PI) on a research project is to show that you have done it before. Do not worry. This is not a rigid requirement because everyone has to get their first funding at some point! However, try building evidence of successfully bidding for small pots of money, for example for travel to conferences, internal funding for events, bidding for time on equipment; this shows proactivity and will help you to develop skills in bid preparation.
- *Papers, journal articles, publications.* The funder will want to know that you have been successful in your research career to date and, rightly or wrongly, academia tends to judge research success based on what and where you have published your research findings.
- *Patents.* Not applicable in every research area but filed patents will be evidence of success in some fields.
- *Other outputs of your research* – performances, software, sculpture, policy recommendations to government. Anything that showcases and provides evidence that you have delivered outputs from the investment in your research is useful.
- *Prizes or awards for your research.* Anything that shows you have achieved success in comparison with your peers demonstrates that enviable quality – esteem. Be careful about providing too much detail though: 'Prize for poster presentation on "The mechanisms of pain in left knees versus right knees" at the International Conference of Great Research, Barcelona, 2019', sounds much better than 'Third prize for poster presentation on …'. Be careful how far back in time you go. Most of the evidence should focus on the last five years. (Do not be tempted to include prizes that you won at school.)
- *Where you have worked and who you have worked with previously.* Rightly or wrongly, the ranking and 'prestige' of the places you have worked in previously will influence the assessor's perception of your research expertise.
- *Media items* – newspaper coverage, blogs (your own, invited posts), v-logs, website. Collect and collate any evidence to support contentions that your research is being communicated and shared.
- *Bibliometrics and altmetrics.* Although not universally loved, if you have evidence that one of your research papers or blog posts has been widely cited and used by others, you can use this as evidence of your impact in your field.
- *Collaborations* – local, national or international. Showing you are connected to the wider research field is an important way to establish yourself as a (potential) leader in your research area.
- *Public engagement activities.* Evidence that you understand the value of two-way communication with the public is especially helpful to demonstrate wide impact.
- *Involvement in departmental/institutional activities* such as being a representative for researchers on departmental or university committees. Provides evidence of your engagement and implies an understanding of the wider issues affecting research and the university sector.

- *Organisation of seminars or meetings*. Such activities show you are a proactive and engaged member of your department/institution.
- *Chair of committees or meetings,* or other *positions of authority*. Such things suggest a level of seniority amongst your peers.
- *Talks or presentations as an invited speaker* at conferences, within your department, or at other universities. Invited talks or keynote presentations infer a level of expertise and high-standing within your discipline.
- *Reviews of journal articles*. Illustrate a level of acknowledged expertise within your discipline.
- *Application reviews*. Any experience of reviewing applications for funding including internal schemes will be helpful to your understanding of the process from the 'other side of the table' but will also demonstrate a level of seniority and respect amongst your colleagues.
- *Conference organisation*. Provides evidence of active involvement in your wider discipline.
- *Member of an editorial board*. This is seen as a measure of esteem in academic circles.
- *Supervision of students or junior colleagues*. Provides evidence of your leadership and management skills.
- *Involvement in mentoring schemes* (being mentored and acting as a mentor for others). Demonstrates your value in investing in your own personal and professional development and that of others.
- *Coordination of projects with multiple partners*. Provides evidence for project management skills and managing diverse people.

This list is not intended to demoralise you! Rather, it is intended to give you a list of things to consider and think about when looking at your CV and considering whether to accept, for instance, any invitation to speak as part of the Faculty seminar series or present a conference paper or review an article. Getting advice from the Careers Service or a Researcher Development team, if available, about developing a balanced CV would be good preparatory work. Keeping your CV updated and taking opportunities to expand your experiences will be beneficial too, not only for your funding applications, but for your career in general.

From the list above, one that is particularly relevant to funding bids and requires attention a long time before you start to write a funding application, is setting up collaborative networks. Collaborations tend to come through maintaining links with former colleagues, via networking effectively at conferences and meetings, and through your network's network, for example someone that your senior colleague personally recommends you contact about a specific technique. (See our sister book *Inspiring Collaboration & Engagement*.) All these relationships are built over time and are long-term projects; potentially one of these contacts could then result in being a collaborator on your bid, seemingly as a by-product of your interactions. Therefore, building your network is an important aspect of academic life in general (**peer review** traditionally being a cornerstone of academia) but with a specific practical relevance for funding bids. Start the process now by engaging with Reflection Point 3.1.

Reflection Point 3.1

Tailoring your network contacts to specific bid opportunities

Consider whether you could use your current network to set up research collaborations for a funding bid. Which of your colleagues might be especially appropriate for each bid you have in mind? (It is always useful to have several potential bids at different stages of preparation.) Might they be considering applying for funding and could you contribute to their proposal and research? This might be a way of getting on the ladder if you have not prepared a bid or had one accepted before.

It is likely that you will use your network to find a host institution for your proposed project. If you will be joining a new research group, department and/ or university then part of your early planning must be around building relationships and understanding of their expertise, structures and working **culture**. This is important because you must show how you and your research will complement and enhance existing streams of work and allow you to establish your own niche. This is especially important when you are making your first steps into independent research and leading your own funded project for the first time. This is much easier if you already have links with the department through your previous networking.

Next you should consider what mentoring, facilities, network of expertise you could tap into to help make your project successful. (See another sister book, *Mentoring to Empower Researchers*.) A funder will want to know that you have considered these aspects of the research environment and the day-to-day practicalities of carrying out the proposed research project. This all adds to the case for your project being viable and feasible. So, while the first consideration of the assessors might be, 'Is this an interesting, important and exciting project within our remit?', the next questions will be along the lines of, 'Is this project feasible within the timeframe and resources requested?' and 'Can this researcher deliver this project?' This is often summarised as the 3 Ps: person, project, place.

To be funded, an application must convince the assessors that it is a great project, the researcher is the right person to carry it out, and the place provides the necessary support, facilities and opportunities to enable success. You can build a relationship with your potential new group by offering to give a seminar or talk.

(From experience, the authors know how grateful people are when someone offers to fill a slot on the departmental seminar series rather than having to deploy a suite of persuasion, negotiation and pleading tactics to complete the schedule.) Arrange to chat with members of the group or department after your talk. If this is not possible, get creative; consider whether you could video-conference or set up a webinar.

Similarly, partnerships with relevant stakeholders such as patient groups, users of your proposed technology, or with industry sponsors, are important to nurture and build ahead of your application. Ask yourself what evidence you have of engagement with stakeholders, or what plans you could put together for doing this as part of your proposed project. This will often link with impact plans or dissemination strategies. (See Voice of Experience 3.1.)

Voice of Experience 3.1

Partnerships with relevant stakeholders

One of us was seeking funding for research on health issues of Asian women so offered a talk about health research to a local Asian women's social and support group. They enjoyed the talk, asked for further contact with the university and not only agreed to participate in the (eventually successful) research project but provided useful information about cultural issues, links to other similar groups and several translators of different Asian languages to help with **participants** whose English was not so good. They later provided help to gain access to other Asian groups for research that colleagues were engaged in and some volunteered to become 'pretend patients' for our Pharmacy students' assessments.

In summary, building up your CV and your network of collaborators takes time and attention, and is something you will need to be doing in advance of preparing a funding application for submission. In the rest of this chapter we will focus on putting together the application document.

Devising a schedule for preparing your application

The first question most people who are new to the world of funding applications asks is, 'How long will it take to put together an application?' One study assessing the time spent on applications to the National Health and Medical Research Council (NHMRC) of Australia estimated the average time to prepare a new proposal to be 38 working days (Herbert, 2013). While this might give you some general indication of the amount of time involved, this result is based on averages and on applying to a specific scheme in Australia so you may still be wondering how long your application will take. There is no definitive answer to this.

There are various tools available for calculating how long a task will take, which are based on estimated times. The bottom-line is these applications always take longer than you will initially estimate or anticipate. Developing an application requires you to become a project manager. You will need other people to be involved with your application and to factor in their inevitable delays at meeting your requested deadlines, and their ability to ignore/misinterpret your requests and emails. Consider the scenario in Example 3.1. Does this sound familiar?

Example 3.1

The frustration of working with others' diaries

Your email (sent on 4th September) to a senior colleague:	Thanks for agreeing to help with the funding application to XXX. Just a reminder that you promised to send me your draft of section 2 by 7th September so that we can discuss when we meet on 12th September.
Reply from senior colleague:	Sorry, I thought you meant you needed the draft by 12th September. I am out of the country and so I don't think I will be able to get this to you until after I am back on 14th September.
You:	OK. Are you still available to meet on 12th September?
Reply from senior colleague:	Sorry. We will need to reschedule that meeting. Please talk with Alex (cc this email, who manages my diary) about finding a suitable time slot.
You (not sent):	Arggghhhh!

Contingency time is important to cover these sorts of scenarios, and the other aggravating scenarios that will mount up during the period you are putting together your application. Perhaps it would be easier if you could do everything yourself, but the reality is that, in order to make your application the best it can be, you will need to involve other people. Putting together an application, even for a piece of work that you may plan to do alone, is not a solo effort. You will need to involve your institution's Finance team, you may require approval from your head of department, and it is vital to get feedback on your proposal (see Chapter 7 on Feedback, and the sister book in series *Inspiring Collaboration & Engagement*).

Preparation time is also a massively important and an often-underestimated part of the application process. By preparation, we mean:

- Doing research on your funder
- Reading all the associated documentation, guidelines and advice
- Finding out who will be reading your application: Does it go to expert reviewers? What is the composition of the review panel? Is there a first stage process that is filtered by scheme managers?
- Checking the assessment criteria
- Looking at previously funded projects
- Talking with people within your institution who have put in bids to your funder of choice.

So, make sure that you factor in time for this aspect of the application preparation. All in all, this means that it is difficult to answer the question of how long it will take. It also follows Parkinson's Law of work expanding to fill the time available for its completion, meaning that you may need to set yourself some artificial shorter deadlines that are robust enough to deter procrastination of the sections you are putting off addressing.

When is the deadline?

Following on from the idea of work filling to expand the time available, you will need to know what time you have available. This may sound obvious, but you will need to formulate a plan based on the final submission deadline (remembering that the final submission may be completed by your institution and not as you hit the submit button), and on the amount of time intervening. The key here is to have a plan and not to just delve in and start doing bits. You will need to set some intermediate deadlines with milestones and deliverables that are agreed with others. For example:

- Prepare the first draft of case for support by 5pm on Friday 21st September.
- Give first draft to Dr Patel-Smith to review and provide feedback on technical content by 28th September (making sure that Dr Patel-Smith is, firstly, willing to give feedback and, secondly, is available to give feedback in this timeframe).

Making the plan

Thus far you have the parameters of your timeline, so you need to think about when you need to incorporate all the important activities.

When choosing where to apply (see Chapter 2) you will have checked the eligibility criteria and details of the funding scheme to which you will be applying. The first part of your plan for putting together your application should include double-checking, even triple-checking, the eligibility criteria. If you are not sure or if you are making assumptions about your eligibility (for instance, 'I assume my two years of working half-time will count as the equivalent of one year in the calculation for the number of years since the award of my PhD') then you must check with your institution's research office (or equivalent), or check with the managers of the scheme at the funding agency to get a definitive answer.

Another part of your plan must include reading all the relevant information you can find on the funder's website about their requirements. The funders are keen to receive good quality, well-written applications from which to choose, so they will often provide comprehensive advice and information about what to include in your application. You should seek out such things as the assessment criteria and the reviewers' handbook. Sometimes these can be lengthy documents, but it is worth the investment of time because by gaining an understanding of what your application is being judged against you can ensure that you address these elements within your proposal. This then makes easier the reviewers' and assessor's job of awarding your proposal a higher ranking according to their prescribed 'marking' scheme. Consequently, this makes your chance of getting onto the 'fundable' pile much greater. In addition to reading relevant online information, talk to colleagues with experience of applying to and working with the funder you will be sending your proposal too. There may be academic colleagues who have acted as reviewers or sat on the assessment **panels** for the funder. They will be able to tell you about any unwritten rules and 'common knowledge' that you could benefit from. It helps to get some insider perspectives and knowledge when interpreting the assessment criteria. Do not be afraid to ask!

Applications will often have the option of attaching **letters of support** or references (see Chapter 5). These can be valuable to your application but will take time and planning to acquire. This may, therefore, be one of the earliest things to organise.

The rest of your plan will include preparing the specific sections of your application as described in detail in Chapter 5. Consider doing the activity in Activity 3.1 to help you consider all the tasks and steps involved, and then arranging them in a logical order. You are likely to go through extensive drafting and re-drafting of the application, and parts of this may be done simultaneously with other steps written on your post-its. However, you are likely to have dependencies such as needing the input of finance team members for preparing the budget and costings before you can prepare the justification for the resources requested. Consider how delays in any of these steps could impact your overall plan.

Activity 3.1

Advice on preparing a plan

- Consider the steps you need to complete for your application.
- Write each step on a post-it note.
- Now, try to put the post-its in order – considering any dependencies (i.e. any steps that must be done before you are able to complete others in the process) and any that can be done simultaneously.
- Use your display of post-its to create a **Gantt chart** for your funding application.

Institutional review and local support

Within your planning, you may need to factor in institutional or internal review processes. Some schemes will have **demand management processes** associated with them meaning that your institution will only be permitted to submit a limited number of applications. This normally means that there is an internal competition ahead of the funders' final application deadline. Your institution may also have quality control processes designed to ensure that only high-quality applications are submitted. These processes are usually in your, the applicant's, best interests too because they are designed to enhance and polish your application. However, they will also have associated deadlines ahead of the final submission deadline.

You will also need to be aware of any timelines that are linked with internal teams such as Research Finance (or equivalent) who may help with costing out your project, dealing with things such as **Full Economic Costings (FEC)** and salary bands. As a rule, the earlier you get them involved in your plans the better. The dedicated people that work in these teams are not usually happy if you only let them know a few days ahead of the submission deadline that you will need their help. They tend to like to talk to you weeks or months ahead of your submission. From experience, it is often good to enter their realm bearing coffee, biscuits or other healthier alternatives.

Check if there are any mentoring schemes (for further information on mentoring see the book in this series entitled, *Mentoring to Empower Researchers*) or programmes designed to help with preparing funding bids. Some institutions have specific schemes to help their early career researchers or those who are putting in large, multi-centre bids. Please see Voice of Experience 3.2 on using internal review processes from an early career researcher.

Voice of Experience 3.2

Using internal review processes

Dr Marianne Coleman, University of Surrey says:

> Peer review is also super helpful – I took advantage of every single internal review process we had, on top of discussing the project idea with my mentors. Getting my statement of career potential reviewed was an especially good plan; we, as early career researchers, can often struggle to sell ourselves, or even to say confidently where the next five years will be taking us. The extra steps I took meant I had a really solid application.

Sticking to the plan

Once you have mapped out all the tasks that need doing, then you need to do them! Sticking to the plan is key, along with managing the timelines of others and factoring in contingency time (i.e. working to 'academic' time). This is not an easy task and is not to be underestimated. The authors sympathise and one (to be unnamed) author has developed a marvellous array of positive procrastination techniques whilst co-authoring this book that all provide legitimate and understandable reasons for not having drafted her chapters as promised ... but the bottom line is that if you want to get the application in (or the book to the editors on time) you will have to write it. Take advantage of whatever motivation tools work for you. Please note, as the article 'Waiting for the Motivation Fairy' by Hugh Kearns and Maria Gardiner (see Further reading at end of the chapter for full details) points out, that if you are reluctant to get started you should not just wait for the Motivation Fairy to fly in! If none of the normal routes are working, try some new ones. Here are some of our suggestions.

Getting started is often the hardest part. One idea to help with this is to practise the '10-minute rule'. You decide to work on a specific task for 10 minutes, which doesn't sound too painful and is certainly achievable for most of us. Once you get started you may be able to do more; if not, at least you have done 10 minutes and next time you won't be starting from nothing. Another tip to help with getting started is, when making your plan, to write down the first small step of each task. This way you will never be sat there thinking, 'So, what should I do first?' This is especially important for the start of the day when (in one author's experience) the temptation of replying to emails and making coffee can significantly delay the start of writing.

Other ideas for helping with the writing part of 'sticking to the plan' include using the Pomodoro technique (see references). The simplest interpretation of this technique involves switching off all distractions including email alerts, social media (children are more challenging!) and working for 25 minutes without stopping and then you *must* have a 5-minute break. Have a drink, a walk, check your emails. Then repeat. You can do this a few times and then have a longer break. There are pre-set timers available online including https://tomato-timer. com/ which can be useful when working on your computer. Additionally, there are apps available designed to either reward you for writing a certain amount of words or to punish you for not. (We always favour the reward approach ... especially cake!)

Knowing you are not alone in your frustrations of filling a blank page* / editing down your masterpiece to fit an obscenely small word count* / having to explain the impact of your amazing research* (*delete as appropriate) can be reassuring and even motivating so signing up for any writing cafes or writing retreats offered by your institution can be valuable. If your institution does not run any, then you could suggest that they be set up, or you could set up your own. Another idea is to get a writing buddy (someone who also has a piece of writing to complete) so that you can check in with each other about how things are going. These check-ins could be pre-set times to phone or email each other to compare how much you have achieved of your pre-determined targets. Another aspect of this idea of not being alone in the process could be to get someone to 'nag' you. This means externalising your deadlines to someone who will ask you about them and check if you have done what you said you will. This could be a colleague, a friend, ... your mum! Whoever will keep pestering you about it so that you would prefer to get the thing done rather than have to explain to them why you have not yet finished!

One final suggestion for helping to stick to the plan is to promise yourself a reward at the end. There can be intermediate rewards along the way but, if there is something significant you have promised yourself for when you are done, you can have that reward in mind when you are secretly cursing that obscenely small word count to describe your amazing ideas.

Attention to detail

Factor in time for proof-reading. Read your text out loud to help you spot overlong or complex sentences. There should be no typographical errors or mis-labelled diagrams with the associated potential to annoy reviewers or panel members. Attention to detail is vital, and you must allow time to ensure that your message is being clearly conveyed to your audience. Panel members often have a large number of applications to review in a short period of time so making your message easy to follow is very important. The style of writing should be consistent and the layout clear and appealing. Pages of densely crammed text are offputting: subheadings, diagrams, highlighting text in bold or italics, bullet point in lists and so on can all aid the reader to pick out the key elements quickly and easily. Panel members report that there is often a very fine line separating bids that are funded versus those that are not, therefore, these seemingly small aspects of your bid preparation can make a big difference. Factor in time to address them.

Stages post-submission

Depending on the scheme that you are applying to, there may be a stage in your application process where you will need to respond to reviewers' comments. The turn-around time for this is usually short and you should have the expected date for this in your diary ahead of time to make sure that it does not clash with when you are planning to explore the depths of the Amazon on fieldwork with no internet access (see Chapter 9, Responding to Feedback). If you know that you are going to be uncontactable or will have difficulty responding on the date the feedback is due, you should inform the funding body and made suitable arrangements. You may also want to check that key mentors who could help you with this vital part of the application are likely to be available at the time you predict you will be asked to respond to feedback comments. If you know in advance that one of your key mentors will be temporarily in a different time zone (for example) during the period that you are likely to need their help, then you (and they) can factor that in or make alternate arrangements.

There may be an interview stage, especially for fellowships, and the time from being invited to the interview can, again, be very short. First, make sure you have the dates for the interviews in your diary; these are usually openly advertised and available ahead of the invitations being sent and, if they are not, it would be sensible to seek advice from the scheme manager or equivalent contact at the funding body. Second, start preparing for the interview at least a few weeks in advance of the advertised interview dates (see section on interviews in Chapter 9). Mock interview panels take time to set up and organise, especially if you want a good range of academics and researchers on your mock panel (which you do!).

This chapter covers a lot of material that is common sense and we hope that it has not come across as patronising. The problem is usually that the simple, common sense things are often forgotten in the excitement of honing complex research ideas. To summarise, we have included below some top tips for planning and managing your application (Top Tip 3.1).

Top Tip 3.1

Planning and managing your application

- Put in groundwork ahead of your application
- Have a plan
- Add in contingency time
- Know who you will need to involve in your plan
- Use strategies to motivate you and help you to stick to your plan
- Use any institutional support schemes
- Factor in time for proof-reading
- Plan ahead for post-submission activities including responding to reviewers' comments and preparation for interview.

In the next chapter we will move on to consider the stages in the application process for three major types of research funding.

Further reading

Herbert, D. L., Barnett, A. G., Clarke, P. and Graves, N. (2013) On the time spent preparing grant proposals: an observational study of Australian researchers. *BMJ Open*, 3: e002800

Kearns, H. and Gardiner, M. (2011) Waiting for the motivation fairy. *Nature*, 472: 127

Pomodoro technique. See: http://pomodorotechnique.com/

4

Stages in the process of submission

In this chapter you will work through:

- Steps to submitting your application, including different stages of the process
- Details of the stages involved in applying for PhD studentships, research fellowships and research grants

Introduction

In this chapter we will consider the submission process for research funding in more detail. First, we will look at the application steps in general terms and then we will focus on the stages involved in applying for three key types of research funding applications: PhD studentships, research fellowships and research grants.

Stages in the application process

The first thing to note is that every funder and every scheme will have their own application process often including their own online submission system that you may need to register for. This application process will incorporate the funder's own specific rules and set of assessment criteria. Furthermore, application processes, rules and assessment criteria are repeatedly being updated and changed. Thus, it is important to check these carefully and ensure that you are using up-to-date information. With this important caveat in mind, we will now look at the usual steps involved in research funding applications.

Most applications will be written and subject to rigid rules, with some schemes also having an interview in addition to the written application (see Chapter 9). The first thing to consider is how many stages there are in the application process. Most written applications are one stage (i.e. one full application is submitted), with some schemes having a subsequent interview for short-listed candidates. However, some schemes operate a two-stage written application process whereby applicants need to submit an '**expression of interest**' (abbreviated to EOI in some instances) or 'intention to submit' form prior to the submission of the full application. These first stage applications will be sifted and assessed and only those that are successful at this stage will be invited to submit a full application. This may extend the length of time for the application process. An example of the timeline for a two-stage application process is shown in Information Box 4.1.

Information Box 4.1

Example of a timeline for a two-stage application process

Expression of Interest (EOI) submission deadline	October
Assessment of EOIs	November
Invitation to submit full proposal	Late November
Full proposal submission deadline	End February
Review	
Assessment panel meeting	June
Interviews (selected applications)	July
Decision	Late July

While it might extend the length of time for the application process, this two-stage system means that there is (perhaps) a more efficient use of time for the applicant, that is, you have got through the first stage before having to write the full and detailed application. For example, the Wellcome Trust Research Fellowships scheme has a 'preliminary application' stage at which they 'assess your eligibility and competitiveness. If suitable, we'll invite you to submit a full application'. However, there is an increase in the administrative steps for the funder when employing a two-stage process, which prompts some schemes to require applicants to submit both parts of a two-step process at the same time, but with the second part only being read if the first section is short-listed.

Another variant of the two-stage process is for longer term funding that is usually associated with clinical research, e.g. the Clinical Research Career Development Fellowships from the Wellcome Trust. This scheme has the opportunity for funding for up to eight years, but this is split into two stages related to the applicant's experience. Stage 1 is designed for early stage postdoctoral researchers looking to establish their research career aims and to gain experience; stage 2 is about making the step to leading an independent research programme and establishing international standing. For full-time researchers each stage can be a maximum of five years, but the total length of the fellowship must not exceed eight years.

The majority of research grants and other research funding schemes operate a single-stage written application system, with some having an interview stage following evaluation of the written proposal for those candidates who are shortlisted. The application is, therefore, usually extensive in its requirements.

Next, we will look at commonly found formats and stages in the application processes for three major types of funding.

Research training grants: PhD studentships

There are different ways to fund your doctorate including self-funding and PhD loans from the governments of some countries; however, in terms of applying for someone else to fund your doctorate, there are two main routes:

1. one is to find a scholarship linked to a specific research project;
2. alternatively, you can apply to an open call from a funder with a proposal outlining your own research idea.

Studentships via either of these routes will typically provide tuition fees and a stipend, and some may cover other project-associated costs such as lab consumables and travel to research conferences, but this varies from scheme to scheme so you will need to check the details.

Like other types of funding, PhD studentships may be available from universities, governmental bodies, private funders such as employers, and charitable trusts. Each will have their own specific application process, but we will look at some of the general stages here.

Where a doctorate is linked to a specific project you are likely to be asked to complete the application form for the institution to which you are applying with stipulations about filling in the title of the project and the name of the project lead as the supervisor for your PhD in the relevant sections of the form.

In the UK, funding from the government for doctoral education tends to come through the UK Research Councils and in recent years there has been a shift to fund and train doctoral students through Centres for Doctoral Training (CDT) or Doctoral Training Centres (DTC) (depending on the discipline). These might be a single university but are usually a group or consortium of universities and industrial partners working together on a priority research area. Students are funded for four years and there is technical and **transferable skills** training included in the programme, as well as carrying out a research project. These programmes tend to be cohort-based with students applying on an annual basis. Many doctoral students find the peer support provided through this cohort-based approach to be particularly valuable in helping them to navigate through their studies at this level.

The application process for this type of funding tends to an open competition that runs annually. Applicants may be asked to apply to the CDT for subsequent placement at one of the partner institutions, or applicants may be asked to apply directly to the host university offering a specific doctoral project. Additionally (and to complicate things further!), there may be separate processes for applying for postgraduate study and for applying for funding, i.e. you might have to apply for a doctoral place separately to applying for the funding to do the doctorate.

The application materials will usually include some of the following:

- Application form
- Research project details
- CV
- References
- Personal statement about your motivation for carrying out a PhD
- English language requirements (**IELTS** score)
- Referees' information

Application forms can be extensive and include many sections. For example, the Techne DTP (Arts and Humanities Research Council funded consortium of universities in London and the South East of the UK) has an application form with the following sections:

- Eligibility check
- Contact information
- Experience, Education and Qualifications
- Duration of study (length of time seeking funding for; part-time or full-time)
- Research Project details
- Resources and Student Personal Statement
- Student's declaration

- References – from two different referees
- Details of Supervisory Team (to be completed by lead supervisor)
- Techne admin information section

For the example above, and in many instances, you will be required to make contact with a potential supervisor ahead of your application. The term supervisor is used in the UK for an advisor, mentor or line-manager for your research work. You can find out more about selecting a suitable university, applying for a doctoral place and making a good start in our sister book: *Fulfilling the Potential of your Doctoral Experience.*

Some doctoral application processes are open to applications all year round, but many schemes have a specific annual deadline. In the UK, these annual deadlines are made in line with students being ready to start their programmes at the beginning of the academic year in late September or early October or the beginning of the Spring term (January) or (infrequently) the beginning of the Summer term (April/May). For institutions working on a semester system there will be other start dates so it is worth checking carefully the systems used in your favoured institutions. Due to the length of time taken to process applications, these begin up to 12 months ahead of that time and often around the January–March before a start date of October. Please see Example 4.1 for an example of a University studentship scheme for funding doctorates.

Example 4.1

Example of a University studentship scheme for funding doctorates

University of Surrey Doctoral College studentships

www.surrey.ac.uk/fees-and-funding/studentships/doctoral-college-studentship-award-2019

If you are interested in applying, please follow the three-stage process below to help you prepare and submit your application.

1. Identify and speak to a prospective supervisor

Within each of the Faculty pages you will find links to academic schools and departments and staff lists. Use the staff lists to identify a prospective supervisor. Contact your prospective supervisor to discuss project options before completing the application. If you have difficulty identifying a prospective supervisor, the Postgraduate Research Director for the department might be able to help you.

2. Apply for a place on a postgraduate research course

Once you have discussed your project with a prospective supervisor you will need to make an application for a place on a postgraduate research course; you can do this through the course page. Please make sure you indicate on your application that you are applying for the Doctoral College Studentship Award (DCSA3). You are also advised to ensure that you include your degree transcripts and references in the application – not providing these documents can slow the process down. The deadline to submit an application for a place on a postgraduate research course is **10:00 GMT 11 January 20xx.**

3.   Complete the Doctoral College Studentships Award application

In addition to applying for a place on a postgraduate research course, you will also need to complete Doctoral College Studentships Award application form. This is your application for funding and will be used to select successful candidates for funding. Please also refer to the guidance notes which will assist you in filling in the application form. Once you have completed your form, please submit it to phdstudentships@surrey.ac.uk by the deadline of **10:00 GMT on 11 January 20xx.**

Following the application deadline, your application will be considered by an academic panel. Candidates will be informed whether they have been successful in securing a studentship award week commencing 18 March 20xx. If you are successful, you will be required to start your programme in October 20xx.

English language requirements
IELTS: 6.5 (with a minimum of 6.0 in each component)

Increasingly, there is an interview requirement associated with such applications so be prepared for that even if you live a distance away because video-conferencing interviews might well substitute for in-person interviews. In some countries, for instance in the USA, some wealthier institutions pay travel expenses and have doctoral recruitment events that may last several days including participation in group events with other doctoral researchers (whose evaluations of prospective doctoral researchers will count).

Research fellowships

Research fellowships are aimed at developing or consolidating a researcher's career. Broadly, three types of research fellowships can be identified: early, mid and senior career research fellowships.

Early career research fellowships are designed for postdoctoral researchers who are usually within a few years after completion of their doctorate. There has been a gradual shift by funders to move from eligibility criteria based on a set number of years since award of the PhD (these would tend to be 3, 5 or sometimes up to 10 years post-PhD award, depending on the scheme) towards a more flexible and inclusive approach that describes the attributes expected of candidates at each career stage or for each type of fellowship scheme.

For example, the UK Engineering and Physical Sciences Research Council (EPSRC) introduced a person specification for their fellowship schemes based on the following attributes: research excellence, setting the research agenda, strategic vision, profile and influence, inspirational team leader, and communication and engagement skills.

Traditionally, early career fellowships are 3–5 years in duration, during which time you are expected to conduct a research project, develop your professional and research profile, and make the first steps towards the establishment of your own academic research group. Recently, in addition to these more 'traditional' fellowships, schemes that are 3–12 months in duration have been introduced by some funders that are designed to consolidate and maximise research outputs and enhance networking and collaboration opportunities for those immediately post their doctorate. Other variants of early career fellowships exist but, generally speaking, all early career fellowship schemes are only open to postdoctoral researchers (i.e. you must have a doctorate or expect to receive the award before the fellowship commences or have equivalent research experience) but not yet hold a permanent position within your organisation. As with all research funding, you will need to carefully check the eligibility criteria and what will be funded (or not funded) as part of the award. Fellowships usually cover a monthly stipend (your salary) and costs for research.

Fellowships are awards that are designed to promote the development of an independent research career and to consolidate the fellow's research area and skills. Fellowships are personal awards and funders are looking to nurture the initial career stages of future research leaders on an international scale. They are an investment in the individual researcher and not just the research project being proposed. The application process for these awards, therefore, tends to reflect these aims and so, if you apply for one of these awards, there will be much more emphasis on you as an individual than for research grant applications.

Here we will look at a generic example based on currently available fellowship schemes.

Steps in submitting an early career fellowship application:

- Submit your preliminary application – this stage is not included in all application processes
- Submit your full application
- Short-listing
- Invited to interview – the majority of early career fellowship schemes have an interview stage

- Application sent out to peer review by external experts
- Reviewer comments sent to you ahead of the interview
- Interview

Sections of the application:

- Title
- Applicant personal details
- Applicant CV/track record/career summary often including a section on how the award of the fellowship will further your career
- **Lay summary**
- Research proposal
- The potential **impact** of your research
- Requested budget
- Head of Department statement
- Statement from mentor or other 'sponsoring' senior colleague
- Letters of support from collaborators and/or referees

As said previously, a fellowship is awarded to the individual researcher and is not just about carrying out a particular research project. This results in the application and interview particularly focussing on your potential as a future research leader, and therefore the section or areas of the application that ask about your future career plans or how the fellowship will further your career are particularly important. For those who are used to working in teams, which is especially common in the sciences and engineering, the language in addressing these sections of the application and answering questions on this in an interview can be challenging because it is natural to say '*we* investigated ...' and '*our* findings show ...'; however, in this context, it is important to show your personal role and involvement and use 'I', 'me' and 'my'. You will find in Chapter 9 some guidelines for preparing for an interview for research funding. Remember that the emphasis for these posts, though, will be on you as a researcher rather than on the particularities of the research project, though they will be included.

Mid and senior career research fellowships will often 'buy out' the time of established academic staff members from teaching and/or administrative activities to allow them to focus on a research project. These fellowships require the applicant to have a track record of independent research, to be carrying out nationally or internationally competitive research, and to be on their way to establishing a profile as a recognised leader in their field. While the application processes will be very similar to those for early career research fellowships, candidates are usually strongly advised to contact the scheme managers at the funding agency to discuss their application prior to submission to ensure eligibil-ity and fit with the funder. Arguably, the most important stages in applying for a senior fellowship are establishing a successful early career stage and raising your research profile and standing amongst your peers, the discipline, and the wider research community. This is where having significant networks with evidence of collaborations and invited presentations beyond your own locality are especially useful so cultivate such opportunities at conferences and by volunteering to serve on committees and so on.

Research grants

The term 'research grants' is a broad definition but is used in this chapter to distinguish them from fellowships. Loosely speaking, and in this context, a research grant can be defined as funding for a discrete research project. The emphasis is placed more on the research work being proposed and this may be car-ried out by a research team with a Principal Investigator (PI) and **co-applicants (co-investigators)** named on the application; whereas in a fellowship appli-cation, the emphasis is balanced more towards the potential of the individual researcher to carry out the proposed research.

There are multiple types of research grants available. For example, there are spe-cific research grant schemes aimed at supporting researchers who are looking to manage their first major research project; as a specific example, there are the UK Economic and Social Research Council (ESRC) New Investigator Grants. There are also Seed funding and pump-prime funds designed to provide researchers with the funds to develop new and untested research ideas. These funds may be used to generate preliminary or pilot data that would support the viability of a larger funding proposal.

The other categories of research grant that you will commonly come across are responsive mode (also sometimes called standard grants) or calls (also called strategic or topic grants). Responsive mode grants support research projects that are open to any research area within the funders' remit. Calls (strategic or topic grants) are focused on a specific topic that is of high impor-tance to the funder. These calls will often be linked to global challenges and strategic priorities. Calls tend to have a short timeframe for submission com-pared with the responsive mode grants that are usually open for submissions at any time (although applications may only be reviewed and funding deci-sions made once or twice a year. Therefore, in practice, deadlines for inclu-sion in each decision panel meeting act as deadlines for submission).

The stages in the process of submitting a grant and its review will vary depending on the funding body. For an example of the steps involved based on the UK Biotechnology and Biological Sciences Research Council (BBSRC) processes please see Information Box 4.2.

Information Box 4.2

Stages in the process of submitting a grant application

- Completed written application submitted via the online submission portal
- Assigned to a Committee
- Application checked for faults and the proposal (sometimes) returned to applicant for correction or withdrawn
- Checked for remit within the funders' strategic aims
- **Introducing Members** (IMs) assigned from the Committee (i.e. two members of the panel are tasked with reading the full and complete application)
- Application sent to IMs
- Sent to expert peer reviewers
- Reviewer's report sent to PI (lead applicant)
- Response to Reviewer's comments prepared by the lead applicant and returned to funder (usually a short turn-around time for this of 1–2 weeks)
- Reviewer's reports and PI response sent to IMs. At this stage the application may be deferred to the following round, that is, to the next Committee meeting
- IMs assess and provide preliminary assessment of the application. Often a scoring system is used to rate the application
- Committee meeting
- Applications discussed and ranked, with individual applications 'introduced' by their IMs
- Committee Chairs' meeting: full ranked list approved and funding cut-off agreed. The number of applications funded may depend on the amount available for that specific round of application and on the requested level of funding from the top applications, i.e. if there is £1 million to give out and the top four applications total this amount, then four awards will be offered. If one of the top four ranked applications has requested a lower amount, then a fifth application may be funded
- PI informed of outcome
- Successful offers prepared and issued, or unsuccessful letter sent to PI
- If successful – grant is accepted by PI and confirmation received from the host institution

It is less common for there to be an interview stage for research grants than in a fellowship application. Please see Information Box 4.3 for an overview of the usual sections in the application form (see Chapter 5 for more details on completing sections of the application).

Information Box 4.3

Sections in the application form for a research grant

- Title
- Lay person or non-technical summary/abstract
- Case for support or project proposal including **aims** and **objectives**
- Budget
- Justification of resources requested
- Lead applicant or Principal Investigator (PI) personal details
- Applicant(s) CV/track record/career summary
- The potential impact of your research. May include a public engagement plan and how you will engage and/or disseminate your research to different stakeholders
- Head of Department statement
- Letters of support from collaborators
- Ethical considerations
- Animal work or Home Office licencing issues for controlled substances
- Data Management Plan (how data will be securely stored, shared, preserved and managed complying with all data regulations and policies. Tools are available – see resources section)
- Cover letter
- Equipment quotations

Other funding sources

This chapter has covered the more 'traditional' and mainstream funding options. However, being open to new collaborations and opportunities is key in these times of political and funding uncertainty. These opportunities may often be small projects or 'pots of funding' but can be valuable in building a track record of funding and offer the potential of future collaboration on larger projects. For example, one researcher was chatting to her surgeon during a minor medical procedure and they made plans to work together to investigate patient experiences of the treatment options with funding coming from the medical institution.

While this approach may not work for everyone, letters of enquiry to businesses and potential industrial partners may be an option for your research area and is something to consider. Universities and Higher Education establishments will often have a team involved with intellectual property, spin-out companies, technology transfer and/or industrial partnerships; they are generally delighted to chat with researchers who are interested in linking to opportunities that they can help to broker. In these instances, the stages of submission will often be less prescribed but will still involve you having a clear project proposal, rationale for the work and budget in a form that meets the expectations of the potential partner.

Conclusion

The stages of submission for research funding can seem onerous but are not uncharted territory, so navigate them using the advice and support of those who have previously sailed these waters. Seasoned explorers are often only too willing to share their expertise, especially when they can provide ideas from their successes to newer recruits.

Further reading

Find a PhD webpages. www.findaphd.com/funding/guides/phd-funding-guide.aspx = comprehensive guide and link to further resources about PhD funding including PhD loans, UK Research Council studentships, university scholarships, Charities and Trusts, and funding to study abroad.
www.findaphd.com/funding/guides/centres-for-doctoral-training.aspx

Data management tools

UK based: https://dmponline.dcc.ac.uk/
US based: https://dmptool.org/

5

Writing each section of the application

In this chapter you will be guided through:

- Practical presentation and writing issues
- Developing an influential argument
- Preparing the case: introduction, rationale and literature review
- Aims, objectives and the consequent hypotheses or research questions
- Describing and justifying research design and methods
- Risk assessment and impact statements
- Corroboration sources: bibliography, referees and support letters
- Preparing synopses: abstracts and lay summaries
- Eye-catching but informative titles
- Covering letter as an extra opportunity

Introduction

In the preceding chapters we have introduced the different types of funding applications and noted that the format differs between funding bodies. However, every funding bid will contain key sections that must be written to indicate that you know what you are doing and will do it well. In this chapter we will present each section, describing the crucial aspects of each. We will, however, reserve one critical section of a proposal for the next chapter – compiling and presenting a budget. Dealing with the financial aspects of research is a tricky issue about which you must liaise with experts in your institution, so it deserves the dedication of a full chapter. The order of presentation in your proposal will depend on the rubric required by the funders while the order of composing and writing each section is not necessarily linear through time. For instance, the title may be the last thing you tackle while the Abstract and Lay Summary must also wait until you have worked through and finalised:

- what you intend to do and why;
- how that translates into answerable research **hypotheses** or questions;
- what **design**, methods and analysis will provide the data to answer them;
- what ethical issues these raise and how they will be addressed;
- how you will deal with any inherent risks;
- and how the research will be evaluated to ensure that the results are meaningful.

Thus, we will present here the sections in the order in which you might address them. We deliberately missed out from that list something that also needs working on – a covering letter. This is sometimes required to accompany your proposal; we will include information about that at the end of the chapter because, in this age of electronic submissions, it is less often required, though when it is, it can be useful. However, while working through this chapter to design your proposal, keep in mind that funding is always limited, and the funders will be expecting clear value for any money they commit. (Note our caveat in Chapter 6 about equally not underestimating costs so appearing too naïve.) There are, though, some other overarching things to decide on first.

Things to consider before you start writing the proposal

To market your ideas effectively, as we discussed in Chapters 3 and 4, you need to have done your homework on the funders who will receive and review your application. Knowing your audience includes choosing the most appropriate tone and language that will impress but not bemuse them. Remember that different people, some who will be experts in your area but certainly not all, will read and pass comment on your proposal so aim to be clear and succinct, addressing an educated generalist. It can be helpful to seek out online or through your research office examples of previous successful applications to determine the conventions used relating to voice (active or passive) and first- or third-person modes of writing. If in doubt, follow the custom and practice in your discipline's most important journals.

Information Box 5.1 provides some practical points for writing.

Information Box 5.1

Practical points for writing

- Keep a dictionary and thesaurus handy to find the most appropriate words.
- Keep paragraphs short and focussed.
- Use headings and subheadings to guide the reader through your story.
- Bullet-pointed lists add brevity and clarity.
- Use diagrams, tables, graphs to summarise points and demonstrate links.
- Avoid jargon, waffle, obscure words and elaborate sentence structures for clarity.
- Acronyms and initials should always be bracketed after spelling them out in full on first presentation.
- Do not use abbreviations commonly used in speech such as 'we'll' or 'don't' or informalities such as 'we are not convinced'.
- Employ italics and bold sparingly, only to make specific points, and avoid underlining entirely.
- Ensure that you use any type face and font suggested by the funders but, if you have a choice, keep it easy to read and consistent.
- Avoid writing in tiny font, annoying to read, in order to cram in more information to a restricted space.
- Check the voice and verb tense traditionally used in applications to this funder.
- Craft your sentences and check drafts assiduously for spelling and grammar.
- Read your almost-ready work out loud to check for sense, convoluted sentences and mistakes of omission and commission.
- Have someone else who will provide honest feedback read your draft before submission to check that it reads well and makes sense.

Remember that producing a well-written, succinct and persuasive argument requires an iterative process, going back and forth to ensure that important points are presented at the right juncture and in a logical order. This always takes time so allow for that when deciding to prepare a funding bid. However, calls for bids frequently require a rapid response. You can be prepared for this by having a stored file of arguments for specific approaches and methods and for **research designs** that you commonly use so that you can tailor them to fit any proposal.

Similarly, you should use referencing software so that you can readily select and convert references to the format required to support your arguments. Some colleagues compile a list of words that are useful in composing an argument (such as: establish, document, demonstrate, reveal, explore, identify, determine, influence, clarify, assess, critique, evaluate, define, discover, appraise, contribute, and so on) to stimulate thoughts.

You may find it helpful, before you start to complete all the sections, to draft out the skeleton of your argument so each section articulates well with others to make sure it all flows smoothly. Reflection Point 5.1 contains questions the answers to which will help you develop your argument for funding.

Reflection Point 5.1

Developing an influential argument

- What is the problem you wish to address through your research?
- What evidence supports the need for this research?
- What are your aims? Your objectives?
- What hypotheses or questions emerge from those aims/objectives?
- What do you intend to achieve and what data do you require for that?
- What approach and methods will yield that data? Why those and not others?
- What research design incorporating these methods will be the most efficient and economical for your circumstances?
- How will you evaluate the success of your research?
- How will you demonstrate the value of your results?
- How will you disseminate your findings?

Let us emphasise here what to avoid when preparing your argument. It is common in other forms of academic writing to set out your argument step by step then conclude – it is the way that we convince those who are as dedicated to our tiny branch of science/arts/humanities as we are because they are familiar with past arguments and the language genre. The gatekeepers who read proposals in the first few 'sifting rounds' are unlikely to be so well-versed in your topic. They will be reading many proposals quickly to identify those worthy of presentation to a committee, therefore they will appreciate it if your writing aids them to see the main points clearly, ready for them to summarise for presentation. One argument form that does this is the 'assert–justify' format in which you start each paragraph with the main message, using the rest of it to convince them that the message is important or true. We have summarised the main benefits of this format in Information Box 5.2.

Information Box 5.2

Benefits of the Assert–Justify mode of argument

The assert–justify mode is useful for funding proposals because:

- Proposals are usually first read and passed on or rejected by administrators who are not familiar with the nuances and vocabulary of your specific research area.
- Speed readers, and those who are tired, bored or lazy, tend to read the first line of every paragraph, skipping from one to the next, looking for something interesting/relevant.
- Important points are readily identified and so easy to summarise.
- A list of main points can be made in preparation for writing the full text.
- Generally, it lends itself to a concise writing style.
- It facilitates the preparation of an introduction or lay summary or presentation by making main points readily identifiable.

Now we can work through each section of your proposal outlining the main content required, starting with what you want to do and why it is an important piece of research. For all the sections that follow keep in mind the specific requirements of your audience, the specific funding body or agency. Many have an application template which you must follow to order your information, and all will have word limits for different sections, each with their own content requirements and titles. Wise applicants familiarise themselves with these rubrics so that they can present the most cogent argument in the required style.

Introduction, rationale and literature review

These three aspects, or similar formulations such as 'background, needs statement and supporting argument/evidence', are all required but can be presented under one heading, separate headings or all subsumed under a heading such as 'Purpose'. They clarify for your readers the topic you have chosen and why you have chosen it, providing the foundation for your research hypotheses or questions. This is where you make the case that this is a worthy study that will contribute something of significance to knowledge and, frequently a requirement currently, to practice. One of our Series authors has provided us with a salutary Voice of Experience (5.1) that relates to the Introduction and to any Abstract you need to include. Consider this before reading on.

Voice of Experience 5.1

Learning to write a compelling 'story'

As a scientist, I have always been taught to write in a very formal, structured way – an introduction that gives the literature background to the project, then the hypothesis or the **research question**, then the **methodology**, then the results, then, finally, a discussion of why the results are interesting. When it comes to writing grant applications, the best advice I have been given is 'write like a journalist, not like a scientist'. Journalists start their piece with the eye-catching headline to get their reader interested, and only at the end go into the mundane detail. This is both to get the reader 'hooked' on the story, and because it may be drastically 'chopped' before publication to make room for another breaking story. When I was first given this advice, back in 2002, the big news story was that the Swedish-born television presenter, Ulrika Jonsson, was having a relationship with Sven-Goran Eriksson, the manager of the England football team. I was told, 'if you were writing about this for a newspaper, you would not begin the story with "Sweden is a Scandinavian country with a population of almost 10 million people...." would you?' Of course not! We need to write our grant applications in the same way. Not sensationalising the story but beginning with the headline news of why the work being proposed is exciting and necessary, and really catch the reader's imagination so that they read on.

An Author/Researcher

This introductory section also demonstrates to reviewers that you are conversant with the field and its literature since you select from the latter those writers whose work is highly respected. This **literature review** must demonstrate a clear need for this project to be done, either to move thinking and practice forward or to solve a referenced problem or to fill a noticeable gap. The size and scope of the literature review will demonstrate to readers that it has been systematically explored and will acknowledge any controversies, indicating its comprehensiveness without including everything written on the subject. You should aim to show that you are familiar with the substantive theories from which you have insightfully selected those most relevant to your purpose.

Few funders are willing to provide financial support for additional literature review although, whether they do fund them or not, they will expect that you keep up to date with new literature as your project progresses. The only exception might be for a project that seeks to explore a very new area using a grounded theory approach to devise theory although often funding is only available for an empirical stage beyond that theory development.

When conducting your review to determine the purpose of your project, ensure that you pay attention also to the approaches and methods used to generate theory and used in related research. Thus, you can be constructing your case for your choice of approach/method at the same time. It may be that either it will be appropriate to use tried and tested techniques or approach the problem from a substantially new perspective. Whichever of those, you will need evidence from the literature to support your contentions in an organised, logical way that builds your position in a convincing way.

All of this applies when you are responding to a call for proposals to conduct an issue already identified by the funders or when you are responding to an open call within a defined subject area or professional context.

Aims, objectives and research questions/hypotheses

Your aims and objectives should derive naturally from your identified purpose but should be couched in a format traditional to that funder. For instance, the aims and objectives may be required at the end of the rationale/literature review or in a separate section. For the rest of this chapter we will assume that you will tailor our advice on content to the requirements of your chosen funder.

Getting the aims and objectives just right is an art and craft because, done well, they provide the reader with a very clear idea of the purpose of the research and exactly what it will achieve while also providing the researcher, you, with a framework to achieve that purpose. The aim should be *clearly and unambiguously* stated to focus on achieving the solution to a *defined, worthwhile* research problem that can *feasibly* be accomplished by using the skills, knowledge and resources of the researcher.

Objectives state the specific activities that will be undertaken so that, taking their outcomes or data together, they will enable you to reach that solution, thus achieving the aim. The number and range of objectives, and perhaps subsequent subquestions, varies but should be reasonably small to ensure that they are all achievable. Usually, objectives are written in the form of a bullet point list prefaced by 'The objectives are:', followed by each objective starting with 'to' do something. They should be precise, well-defined and tangible. The opposite, what not to do with aims and objectives, is exemplified in Activity 5.1.

Activity 5.1

Reviewing aims and objectives

Consider the following aim:

This project is intended to explore the value of training of First Responders in healthcare.

WRITING EACH SECTION OF THE APPLICATION | 71

Before reading further, think about the clarity and ambiguity of this aim, what research problem it might be the consequence of and how feasible it might be to accomplish. What objectives might derive from it?

On the surface anything that relates to training others in healthcare would seem to be a worthwhile activity. However, value is something, like beauty, that is in the eye of the beholder. Are the beholders here the Responders, the patients, the Health Service or the public at large? What constitutes value for each of those people/groups? Do they already have training, of what kind and what would constitute the training under investigation? And can we presume that the results will be applicable to all Responders or only a specific group in a defined healthcare context. Lots more questions might be asked of this aim, which then would impact on what objectives might be derived from it.

Subject your own aims to this kind of scrutiny before developing your precise, well-defined and tangible objectives.

The first thing to think about for the next stage is whether the results of your objectives, which serve to ask the generic question 'what is happening?', will result in data that answers questions such as 'how or why', or 'how many, how much, how far, big, etc.' It is likely that for the how and why questions you will need to formulate *research question/s* the answers to which will be mostly, if not all, in the form of **qualitative** data. Thus, your research will be embedded in an interpretative framework or philosophical approach or **paradigm**.

If your data consists mainly of numerical or **quantitative** data, as for questions about how many, how much, etc., then you should derive a hypothesis and its contrast, a **null hypothesis**.

The approach or paradigm in these cases will be the **neo-positivist** paradigm which lends itself to statistical analysis techniques to judge the probability of results answering the null hypothesis. Please note that the two over-arching paradigms are sometimes, indeed frequently, erroneously called the qualitative and quantitative paradigms respectively although only data can really be described by these terms and any research project could use methods that produce one, the other or both kinds of data. Bear in mind also the other following important points:

- Different paradigms tend to be suitable for different contexts and discipline areas.
- Interpretative research leads to research questions while neo-positivist research requires hypotheses.
- Different data collection methods as well as different data types typify each paradigm.

Like objectives, both research questions and hypotheses need to be carefully structured to be clear and specific. As you will have found from formulating objectives in Activity 5.1, framing unambiguous questions that will produce the information required is a complex task, just as is 'operationalising ' your hypotheses to ensure that they can be effectively tested. In case you are relatively new to research in your discipline domain, we will provide at the end of the chapter reference to several books that provide more detailed descriptions of how to produce the kinds of aims, objectives, questions and hypotheses that will impress reviewers of your project as well as guide your research design and methods.

Research design and methods

The design of your research project and the methods you will use to collect data are intimately intertwined together and should fit neatly within your preferred paradigm. The data that will answer questions or support/negate hypotheses should be collected and analysed in a way which is internally consistent, that is, the tools used to gather and investigate data respect the parameters of the paradigm, which itself is indicated by the kinds of questions asked. A paradigm, briefly, is the set of values and beliefs that orientate research, the kinds of questions it asks and the approach and methods chosen to address them. It is important also to ensure that your language is consonant with the paradigm within which you intend to work: for instance, in neo-positivist research proponents refer to human contributors as **subjects** whereas in interpretivist approaches they are more usually referred to as participants; similarly, while the **validity** and **reliability** of data is crucial for neo-positivists, for interpretivists its **authenticity** is paramount.

Whatever your discipline and paradigm of choice, turning a great idea into a feasible and productive research project design needs a great deal of care and attention not simply for ensuring that the project works but to convince others of its viability, that it will do what you contend that it will. It is worthwhile drawing up a long version of the design/methods that contains all the detail to guide your work (and to ensure you can answer questions of detail should you be interviewed) and then condensing it into its essential framework to fit required word constraints. If the latter are very tight you may be able to use a 'technical detail' appendix or at least provide a reference to published work (preferably yours) that provides more detail. What the funders will be looking for in any proposal is a clear, organised, logical presentation about how you plan to conduct your **experiments**, **surveys**, reviews, text analysis, secondary data analysis, or model testing, whichever is appropriate. We present the main aspects of a methodological argument in Information Box 5.3.

Information Box 5.3

Important items in the methodology section

After noting the general paradigm which orientates your project, you should include the following:

- The methods to be implemented, when, how and why.
- How you will develop or refine **instruments** and how they will be used, including a justification for their selection over other possibilities.
- Your selection criteria and how you will access or recruit your **sample**, again with justification, if sampling from a **population** of some kind forms part of the project.
- A timeline within which you indicate key milestones and how different stages of the research articulate with one another, perhaps using a Gantt chart.
- Some form of risk assessment information that both recognises that sometimes things do not go to plan and provides contingency plans.
- A discussion of the **credibility** of the expected data (validity, reliability or authenticity, replicability/reproducibility) and how it will be analysed, including what tests will be used if appropriate.
- What data interpretation procedures you will use and their relevance.
- Ethical considerations and how they will be achieved, including any permissions, either already acquired or to be sought. (Remember to factor in enough time for **ethics** agreements, which can be dependent on meeting dates of Ethics Committees, if required – and they often are.)
- Project management or research governance information, for instance, who will lead the project, how different packages of work will be determined and allocated, and how you will ensure that time is managed effectively. Work package allocation and time management are both things that are particularly important in large-scale projects.
- An evaluation strategy to show how you will assess the value or impact of the project, its output and potential outcomes, in other words how well the objectives and the research aim have been achieved.
- A dissemination strategy might be required in this section or as a separate section, but it is important to promote impact of all kinds: academic, professional, public and economic.

The items listed in Information Box 5.3 apply even if your research is intended to take an **iterative design** with each succeeding stage determined by the data from the preceding stage, as you might in exploratory research projects. You should present a rationale for a range of options that you have considered in advance albeit that these might be in a generalised form to be refined in the light of the resulting data.

In relation to research methodology there are some key words that occur frequently here and in other literature on how to succeed in writing up your research plans or project reports. These are 'justification', 'credibility' and 'evaluation'. These are critical in and for any research, in the sense of being vitally important and in the sense of carefully assessing value. They apply equally to the choice of project purpose and to the whole methodology section because there is a myriad of questions one could pose about any area and there is a wide selection of approaches and methods that one could use to explore it.

Reviewers want to know why you decided to select your specific topic and will expect you to defend rigorously all your choices about how to do so. Every time you make a selection or come to a decision then ask yourself 'why', what evidence supports that choice. You can add to that defence using the literature and other people's corroboration of your research skills and knowledge, all of which we discuss in the next main section. First though, let us look at the oft-neglected aspect of risk assessment and the increasingly important 'impact statements'.

Risk assessment and impact statements

When bidding for funding for a project that is dear to your heart it is easy to forget that there are a multitude of other potential projects competing for the same pot of gold. For every project funded there is an 'opportunity cost' related to those not so lucky. Thus, the managers of those funds have a responsibility to ensure that the money is well-spent, that is, has been allocated to a project that is likely to meet its aims and produce something (usually data and conclusions) that is in some way valuable.

They will be more convinced that your project is likely to meet its aims if you can demonstrate that you have evaluated the potential risks to your successful completion and have contingency plans ready with which to reduce their effect on the outcomes. You will find it useful to make yourself a list of all the potential hazards, things you can think of that might go wrong. This could include unavailability of people (colleague co-contributors and respondents), resources, kit, specific chemicals or bugs or similar, for all sorts of reasons such as strikes, government policy, weather, and no end of other calamities including fire, flood and pestilence. Then consider how you could manage without them or obtain a suitable substitute. Once you are conversant with all the potential pitfalls, condense them into a concise paragraph noting the main potential risks, your evaluation of their likelihood and how you would best manage them to save the project and maintain its potential impact.

A requirement for an **Impact Statement** is becoming more frequent but even if it is not explicitly required you should emphasise the value of your outcomes, demonstrating that your project will provide identifiable value for money in the form of contributions to academia, the professional world and for society by enhancing theory, practice, health, the economy, the environment, and so on. Further, you should be clear about who will benefit from this research for there are multiple possible levels of impact, for instance it may assist at the individual, organisational, community or social level. A combination of these would strengthen your proposal as would careful attention to the aspects we discuss next.

Bibliography, letters of support and referees

Your bibliography or reference list not only supports your specific choices but also demonstrates your ability as a researcher and your knowledge of the field. In that section you can display your skill in selecting, from all those texts (articles, books, reports, public documents) those which are most germane to your topic. You must show that you know the current relevant theories and state of the art processes through your citations. Therefore, since word counts are strict, and succinctness valued, you must resist the temptation to show off that you have read everything in the field, instead selecting the 'precious' few that will provide the best support for your arguments.

There are several situations in which letters of support can be crucial for obtaining funding. These include the need to gain access to a specific context, say a school or hospital or another research facility or private or restricted access library or museum. Another such situation is when you require as participants/subjects groups of people with special knowledge, such as employees or experts or members of a specific group, and this is particularly important if they might be vulnerable in some way, such as children or patients. Another group for whom a letter of support might be reassuring is public or well-known figures, sometimes known as expert witnesses, who may be nervous about sharing their views in public. Letters of support in these instances should come from gate-keepers, those in positions of influence who are respected both by potential participants and the research community.

Indeed, you may be intending to work with other members of the research community on a collaborative project, in which case you will need letters of support that confirm commitment to the project and that detail how that collaboration will work, how much of it there will be (including the use of time, equipment and other resources), and why it is being undertaken. In all these letters of support a convincing case must be made for the project itself and for you undertaking it, so if the letter author is not familiar with the funders' requirements you should provide clear guidance about the general style and content required.

Your referees will also want to see any letters of support, so you need to plan carefully the order of preparing your proposal, seeking preliminary tentative and then strong approval from those providing support letters. We include tentative agreements so that you do not waste time preparing a detailed proposal before you know if you can, for instance, gain critical access, so it is worthwhile seeking provisional approval and then later firm commitment from your referees.

You may, depending on the funder, be allowed or required to select your referees. Be careful to select people who are genuinely independent of your research because those with whom you have worked closely or from your own institution will be discounted. They should be, though, able to make a fair but rigorous assessment of your past research and your research potential while being recognised experts in the general field addressed by your project. It is important that you gain their permission to nominate them not simply because it is good manners to do so but also because, otherwise, they might refuse to respond to any request from the funder, leaving the funder either to seek someone else, perhaps less au fait with your work, or to reject your proposal out of hand.

So now your proposal is almost prepared – it merely needs to be summarised in two forms. We stay 'merely' rather tongue in cheek because these are demanding tasks as you will see from the next section.

Abstract and Lay Summary

It is sensible to prepare your Abstract and Lay Summary once you have developed the full proposal because often initial 'good ideas' become refined and developed as you write, and you will then have a fuller picture of the complete project (see the article by Walter Ong in the Further reading section at the end of this chapter). The Abstract is read early in the selection process by 'gatekeepers' and so it is vitally important that you capture their attention so that they are seduced into reading the rest, and then use your Abstract to present your proposal to any decision-making committee. If it is not compelling, then it is likely that your proposal will fail at this juncture. It will not be compelling if it is not clear and well-written or if it fails to obey any directions given by the funder. Thus, when designing your Abstract first check how many words you are allowed by the funder. Frequently, these range between 200 and 300 so it is quite a task to condense your research proposal into an Abstract that covers the main points in the form of an executive summary:

- The argument for the topic of the study;
- What aims it intends to achieve and why;

- How it intends to achieve those aims: the conceptual framework and the methodology;
- The expected results and their potential impact (your 'unique selling point' or USP).

Thus, the art of Abstract writing is to convey as much as possible as succinctly as possible. We suggest that you draft your Abstract then revise it to eliminate all unnecessary words such as adjectives/adverbs that are merely decorative, then revise it with the help of a thesaurus to use one (distinctly appropriate) word to replace phrases. However, then check that you have used vocabulary that any educated person would understand, avoiding too technical terms. It is important that your Abstract stands out in the crowd because it has something special to offer that is readily understood. (By the way, we have already passed the 300-word limit since the beginning of this section.)

Having prepared your Abstract you should then be prepared to translate it carefully into a Lay Summary, which is increasingly being required by funders. This is in acknowledgement of the money generally being provided by the public purse and so they, the public, have every right to know what it is being spent on. If you have crafted your Abstract well, then you should be able to amend it into a lay-person accessible form by eliminating any 'research professional' words by replacing them with equivalent words that you would find in any quality national newspaper. One of your authors always suggests that you should then send it to the equivalent of her mother, an intelligent someone who is not in an academic community, to check that they understand your intent and find it interesting.

Both these sections should follow and elaborate on your well-constructed and evocative title, which we turn to next.

The importance of the right title

We like to suggest that your title should be precise, concise and elegant – and it is no mean feat to achieve that, especially using accessible language that attracts further reading. Bear in mind, though, the audience for this document. It is not one seeking a mystery, or an adventure book or film, so avoid 'clever' titles that play on words. Since many funders require your title to be restricted to quite a small number of characters (sometimes these include spaces too) then you need to capture only the essence of your research project. Thus, you should avoid superfluous phrases such as: 'A Project to …' or 'An Investigation of …' and certainly any emotive words and punctuation such as exclamation marks. Simple is best. At this point it might be useful to engage in Activity 5.2.

Exploring the format of proposal titles in your discipline

You may find it helpful to check the titles used in recent successful projects supported by a range of funding bodies that fund research in your own disciplinary area, analysing them for common features and structures.

How succinct are they? What key words are used frequently? Practice this craft by considering how any of your previous research projects could be encapsulated in a similar form.

Covering letters

Since most funding bodies now require electronic submissions the opportunity to use a covering letter is infrequent. However, if such an opportunity arises and, indeed, when one is requested, then use this to your best advantage by ensuring that your passion for research, and this project in particular, shines through the relatively formal style required. Make sure that it creates a good impression by paying attention to presentation: layout, font, tidiness, and is addressed to a specific named person, using the correct title (check the website or phone the secretary of the organisation).

Compose the main body of the letter by first stating your credentials and your purpose in writing, followed by anything you want to draw special attention to in your proposal (for instance, why you are especially well-placed or well-qualified or well-experienced to undertake this project) in a brief statement that demonstrates that you are conversant with the organisation's mission and interests (which you will already have found from the website!). You can, for instance, use a phrase such as 'noting your interest in' or 'Being aware of your support of projects in this area'. Then note any enclosures (your CV and proposal perhaps) so that they do not get lost or overlooked between reviewers and sign off politely but not effusively. Remember that short and sweet is a preference in any business.

The next important section of the proposal

Of course, in preparing your proposal you will have been careful to ensure that it can be achieved within a reasonable budget. We have devoted a whole chapter, Chapter 6, to this critical section and it is worth reading that before firming up your main draft of the proposal so that you can ensure that everything you want to include will be recognisable as value for money.

As a summary of this chapter, we refer you to Top Tip 5.1.

Top Tip 5.1

Criteria by which to judge your proposal

- Are you clear about what your research will address?
- Have you provided a cogent argument about why it is important?
- Have you demonstrated that its output and eventual outcomes will be useful?
- Have you shown that this funding is necessary to complete the project, rather than coming under the purview of your institution or industry?
- Does your literature review demonstrate the originality of the research as well as its relationship to other research in the field?
- Have you justified compellingly that the aims, approach and methods will provide a substantive outcome?
- Does your research plan persuade readers that the project can be efficiently completed within the given timescale?
- Have you assessed the risks and included a contingency plan?
- Will you be using appropriately compatible analysis and interpretation methods?
- Is the project explained as cost effective?
- Do you have an evaluation and dissemination plan?
- Is your proposal convincing to lay people as well as experts?

Further reading

Books on research proposal writing

Berry, D. C. (2010) *Gaining Funding for Research: A Guide for Academics and Institutions*. Maidenhead: Open University Press (UK funding orientated)

Carlson, M. and O'Neale-McElrath, T. (2008) *Winning Grants: Step by Step*. San Francisco, CA: Jossey-Bass (USA funding orientated)

Coley, S. M. and Scheinberg, C. A. (2008) *Proposal Writing: Effective Grantsmanship*. Thousand Oaks, CA: Sage (USA funding orientated)

Day, P. A. (2003) *Winning Research Funding*. Aldershot: Gower (UK funding orientated)

Denicolo, P. M. and Becker, L. (2012) *Success in Research: Developing Research Proposals*. London: Sage (Mainly for research design and methods and lists of funding sources and of resources)

Punch, K. E. (2000) *Developing Effective Research Proposals*. London: Sage (Mainly for research design and methods and examples from the Australasian context)

Books on research methodology: general

Gray, D. E. (2009) *Doing Research in the Real World* (2nd ed.). London: Sage

Kumar, R. (2011) *Research Methodology: A step by step guide for beginners* (3rd ed.). London: Sage

Locke, L., Silverman, S. J. and Spirduso, W. W. (2004) *Reading and Understanding Research* (2nd ed.). Thousand Oaks, CA: Sage

Ong, W. J. (1986) Writing is a technology that restructures thought. In: Gerd Baumann (Ed.), *The Written Word: Literacy in Transition*. New York: Oxford University Press.

Patton, M. Q. (2002) *Qualitative Research and Evaluation Methods* (3rd ed.). Thousand Oaks, CA: Sage

Rumsey, S. (2008) *How to Find information: A guide for researchers* (2nd ed.). Maidenhead: Open University Press

Books for different disciplines

Ackerson, L. G. (Ed.) (2007) *Literature Search Strategies for Interdisciplinary Research: A sourcebook for scientists and engineers*. Lanham, MD: Scarecrow Press

Adams, l. S. (1996) *The Methodologies of Art: An introduction*. New York: Icon Editions

Black, T. R. (1999) *Doing Quantitative Research in the Social Sciences*. London: Sage

Clifford, N. and Valentine, G. (Eds.) (2003) *Key Methods in Geography*. London: Sage

Cohen, J. and Medley, G. (2000) *Stop Working & Start Thinking: A guide to becoming a scientist*. Cheltenham: Stanley Thornes

Cohen, L., Manion, L. and Morrison, K. (2011) *Research Methods in Education* (7th ed.). Abingdon: Routledge

Daymon, C. and Holloway, I. (2010) *Qualitative Research in Public Relations and Marketing Communications* (2nd ed.). Abingdon: Routledge

Fellows, R. F. and Liu, A. (2008) *Research Methods for Construction*. Chichester: Wiley-Blackwell

Flowerdew, R. and Martin, D. (Eds.) (1997) *Methods in Human Geography: A guide for students doing a research project*. Harlow: Pearson-Prentice Hall

Harner, J. L. (2002) *Literary Research Guide: An annotated listing of reference sources in English Literature Studies* (4th ed.). New York: Modern Languages Association of America

Holmes, D., Moody, P. and Dine, D. (2006) *Research Methods for the Biosciences*. Oxford: Oxford University Press

McDowell, W. H. (2002) *Historical Research: A guide*. London: Longman

6

Getting to grips with finances

Guest co-author: Phil Lidiard

In this chapter you are introduced to:

- The first steps in costing a proposal
- Research accountability
- Core rules for costing any research project
- Key elements when preparing a budget

Introduction

Getting the costings right is fundamental for a successful proposal. No research project is cost-free including those projects that may involve only you and your computer, and you will have to give careful consideration to this section in the application even if you are applying for a small amount of money. Before developing the costings of your proposal, you need to be clear about the research you want to do, how you will do it, and what you will need.

The reasons for costing your research proposal might seem obvious to you but, often, preparing the **costs** are seen as one of the most challenging parts of the process which is understood only by financial experts. However, rest assured, even though you will have to be familiar with the financial aspects of a research proposal, there is also expert advice available in your institutions to help you through the whole process. If you are preparing a proposal seeking funding for doctoral study you will not be expected to be fully conversant with all the financial issues related to research but it will help your case if you demonstrate awareness that no research is cost-free and have some notion of the aspects that need to be financially accounted for in a research project. Therefore, we provide some insights into the key concepts and the process of costing for anyone planning to submit a research proposal to any funder.

The first steps to costing a research proposal

Although costing a proposal may vary from funder to funder, there are some general rules that we recommend you follow when preparing your research budget. Here, we do not intend to be exhaustive but to provide you with some essential steps that will help you to get your costings right. We suggest that you contact your research support office and other senior colleagues for additional and more targeted advice when preparing your costs for a specific project.

Most important: read the funder's guidance

Arguably a very important step when preparing a research proposal is to thoroughly read the funder's guidelines including the costings section. By reading the guidance notes you will understand exactly what the funder wants to see in your application, after which you can make sure your application addresses all the points and activities required.

All funding schemes have clear guidelines on their remit, the aims of the call and the costs allowed in your proposal and you are expected to adhere to these criteria. These guidance notes will invariably prompt you to consider some costs you might not have thought of when developing your research, and they will also explain what the funding limit is (minimum and maximum funding amounts) and what they are willing to pay for (eligible costs). The funder will also provide a point of contact with whom you can discuss your project and clarify some points.

Although each funder has its own forms and requirements regarding eligible costs, there are some terms that are shared by the majority of them and understanding what these terms mean is crucial (see Information Box 6.1; this is an augmented version from Denicolo and Becker, 2012, p.80).

Information Box 6.1

Common definitions related to research budgets

Co-Investigator: This researcher has some level of joint responsibility, with the PI, for the project in terms of its management and intellectual leadership.

Cost: How much conducting your project will cost your institution.

Directly allocated costs: Some resources used by a project may be shared with other projects or research activities; for instance, the running costs of equipment or the costs of bulk orders. An estimate of the proportion of the cost applicable to the funded project is made and this is charged as an allocated rather than directly incurred cost.

Directly incurred costs: These are identifiable costs evidenced by an **audit record** of invoices and receipts that can be traced as specifically arising from the conduct of the research and are debited from the grant as the actual cash value.

Full economic cost (FEC): This is the total cost, which includes direct and indirect costs and an overhead cost, as well as a contribution to a recurring investment in the research institution's infrastructure.

Grant: This is the common term for the financial support of a project which tends to cover only a proportion of its full economic cost. **A research grant** is the term used to denote the financial contribution made towards a research project by a funding organisation using its own assessment procedures and criteria.

Grant holder: This is the individual who is allocated the grant and who has intellectual and managerial responsibility for it. The common name for this person is Principal Investigator or PI.

Indirect costs: This is a calculated proportion of a range of costs that are charged to all projects that have not been otherwise included in the directly allocated costs, and which may include the costs of departmental or institution-wide administration and services such as library and IT Departments.

Personnel on-costs: This is an additional cost that your employer will have to cover when employing someone, such as an occupational pension scheme and national insurance costs.

Price: How much you request or eventually get from the funder.

Research organisation: This is the organisation which employs the PI and which is responsible for the administration of the awarded grant. The majority of funders will require the PI to be employed by a research organisation at least for the duration of the grant.

Virement rules: It refers to the transfer of one budget line to another. Most funders will provide you with the opportunity to re-allocate funds albeit subject to certain limits. For instance, you may not need to use all your budget allocated for travel (you might get a cheaper fare) but might be allowed to vire the remainder over to accommodation (if more expensive accommodation is available) or to equipment (if a more effective but more expensive piece of kit becomes available).

It sometimes comes as a surprise that you should include in your costing the use of university facilities but, at least in the UK currently, an important part of research income is its contribution to infrastructure and facilities. You can understand that it is similar to accounting for 'wear and tear' or depreciation of your car so that you need to set aside money to replace it. Running a university is more complex than running a car so it is wise to seek the help of experts.

Talk to your research support office and senior colleagues

We have already mentioned in previous chapters that it is advisable to discuss your proposal with more experienced colleagues who will give you feedback on the proposed research project, such as its design and viability, and we will elaborate in Chapter 7 on the nature and value of that feedback and how to use it effectively. However, remember that they can also advise on the types of cost and funding levels you ought to be seeking in your proposal. Investigating your organisation's costing criteria and the resources already available will be important too.

We recommend that you get in contact with your research support office or costing team in your organisation as early as possible since there are an almost endless array of rules and policies surrounding costs for research such as: the funder's eligible costs, funding rates, value-added tax (VAT), your employer's Human Resources rules, exchange rates and inflation rates, and many others. The sooner you contact them, the more time they will have to go through the costings with you and get them right.

Your research support office (or similar) will do most of the calculations for you but it is important that you understand what they do and how you can help them so they can produce an accurate cost for your proposal. It is also useful to contact your IT and facilities specialists in your institution if you are including equipment or require additional space/facilities for your proposal.

Justification of costs and research accountability

All funders will expect that you clearly justify all costs included in your proposal. Justifying the reasons behind each item/concept included in your proposal (e.g. salary, equipment, travel, etc.) and demonstrating that your research is well worth the money spent on it (value for money) is essential for a successful application.

Costs should be realistic because people reviewing your proposal have a wealth of experience and they will have a good insight into the level and types of funding you are requesting. You will have to convince them that you have given serious thought to the financial aspects of your proposal and that you have not underestimated or overestimated costs.

You will also need to demonstrate that any commodity included in your budget is not already available in your organisation and, further, that without it you will not be able to achieve the aims of your proposal. For example, you would not be expected to include budget to cover a laptop that is similar to those that your Department supplies to all staff but you could request budget to buy a high-powered laptop that is essential for the storage and retrieval of large quantities of information and that is not available in your Department.

This is the essence of research accountability and getting it wrong may signal to the reviewers that you are inexperienced, thus leading to doubts in their mind about your ability to conduct your project and to produce the expected outputs from your research. A well calculated and justified budget shows good planning and attention to detail which strengthens your overall application making it more likely to succeed. Of course, each funder has a limited budget and so you might think that if your project seems inexpensive, then it might encourage them to fund it. However, on the contrary, they will not want to invest their money in one that is likely to fail because it has been under-funded. Equally, your institution is not likely to support a funding bid that will lose it money, except in very exceptional cases such as those that compensate for financial loss by considerable gain in prestige. Even then, your internal negotiation skills will be strongly tested.

Test drive your ideas at an early stage

It is good practice to 'test drive' your ideas with the help of your costing specialists to see if the scope of your proposed activities satisfies the funder's rules. An early 'test drive' of some preliminary cost ideas can be very useful in identifying if your project's scope is in line with the funder's expectations. This will avoid future disappointment and you will not waste time preparing a really detailed, well-written proposal to later learn that you have, for example, exceeded the maximum funding amount allowed so that you will have to adjust your proposal with little time available before the funder's closing date.

Funding and spend

Being successful with a funder does not mean that you will receive the requested funding in one single payment but rather you get it in arrears. That is, you must spend it first and invoice the funder for the actual costs. For example, if you said that you were going to spend £700 on travel to meet your collaborators in another country but you actually spent £500, the funder will only pay £500. This is important because you (via your institution) will not get the funding until you have spent it and you will have to send the funder receipts for the costs incurred so that your institution can recover that cost.

Costing and pricing

One of the important things you will need to understand for the finances of a research funding application is the difference between *costing* and *pricing*. The cost of a research proposal is how much conducting your project will financially cost your institution including all aspects; for example, not just the cost of the specific laboratory consumables and time on the equipment you might need for your planned experimental work but also the cost of the electricity to run the machines and the cleaning of the office you work in. UK universities, for example, have to apply the rules of *Full Economic Costing* (*FEC* or *fEC*) when calculating the cost of a project. This concept was introduced in September 2005 to ensure that UK universities were monitoring the true cost of their research and recover that cost. Your research support office can help you understand these and other related concepts when preparing your proposal.

Once the cost has been calculated then the funding amount (otherwise known as the price) can be identified. In simple terms, the price is how much you request or eventually get from the funder. Whilst the cost of your proposal remains constant, the price will vary from funder to funder. The price may be below, equal or (rarely) above the full cost of the research. Information Box 6.2 shows an example illustrating how a single cost for a research project can generate different prices or requested funding amounts depending on the rules of the funder, such as how much they are willing to pay for certain aspects, if they will pay for them at all.

Information Box 6.2

Differences between cost and price (disregarding inflation applications)

Cost type	Full Economic Cost (FEC) £	Funding (Price) UK Research Council £	Charitable Trust £	European Council £	Industry £
Postdoctoral Researcher (staff)	125,000	100,000	125,000	125,000	125,000
Consumables	20,000	16,000	20,000	20,000	20,000
Travel & subsistence	10,000	8,000	10,000	10,000	10,000
Other costs	10,000	8,000	10,000	10,000	10,000
Sub-total	165,000	132,000	165,000	165,000	165,000
Salaries – Researcher PI / Co-I	30,000	24,000	0	30,000	30,000

	Full Economic Cost (FEC)	Funding (Price)			
		UK Research Council	Charitable Trust	European Council	Industry
	£	£	£	£	£
Overheads					
Estates	25,000	20,000	0	0	25,000
Direct allocated costs Infrastructure	3,000	2,400	0	0	3,000
Indirects	120,000	96,000	0	0	120,000
Funder flat rate overheads	0	0	0	48,750	0
Sub-total	148,000	118,400	0	48,750	148,000
Total	**343,000**	**274,400**	**165,000**	**243,750**	**343,000**
Funding as a % of FEC		**80%**	**41%**	**71%**	**100%**

When reading the funder's guidelines make sure that you and your research support office are aware of the type of costs they are prepared to fund and how they will want you to present the budget. Some funders may prefer an itemised budget (a line for each item of costs and separated by personnel and operational costs) whereas others may require a functional budget (which aggregates expenditure under each research objective).

Key types of costs for research funding

The following represents a general array of types of cost for research funding. However, applicants will need to refer to the specific funder or scheme guidance to confirm the approach to specific types of cost; for example, some funders may not fund travel expenses or may limit the amount of time a PI can cost in the project.

Staff or personnel costs

The largest part of your budget's direct costs will often be the cost of employing staff, although this will depend on what type of project you are intending to undertake. Staff costs will be higher than just the basic salary since you will also need to take into account your employer's extra costs, known as on-costs. The two largest such on-costs are frequently your employer's contribution to an occupational pension scheme and national insurance costs or other national equivalents. Together these can add approximately 30% to the basic salary, a percentage that will rise as the basic salary rises.

Other factors to take into account will be: area weightings (for example, in the UK there is a London Allowance due to the higher cost of living in the capital city), your institution's policies for increments (regular salary rises that will occur over the life of the project) and inflation and starting grades, the duration of the post, whether the post-holder will be full-time or part-time, your choice of starting grade for the post, and so on. Information Box 6.3 attempts to illustrate the full cost of an individual postdoctoral researcher and how these costs might rise over the course of a three-year project.

Information Box 6.3

An example of how to calculate staff costs

If you want to employ a Postdoctoral research staff member full-time for 3 years on a salary of £30,000 per annum, you may think that this will be a total of £90,000 in your budget on the funding application. As you will probably be already aware, it is not this straightforward because there are other costs that need to be considered when employing people. The £30,000 is just the start. The following is a rough illustration of the cost of employing a Postdoctoral Research Assistant full-time for 3 years starting on a basic salary of £30,000:

Salary per year	Cost	Subtotal per year
Year 1 basic salary	30,000	
employer on-costs	9,000	
subtotal		**39,000**
Year 2 basic salary	31,200	
employer on-costs	9,360	
subtotal		**40,560**
Year 3 basic salary	32,500	
employer on-costs	9,750	
subtotal		**42,250**
Total cost for 3 years	**121,810**	**121,810**

The above costs assume an annual increment for the Postdoctoral research staff member up to the next grade, a modest inflationary pay rise each year, and employer on-costs equivalent to 30% of the basic salary. You may have to consider **overheads** too and this can increase the cost of a Postdoctoral researcher even further.

Overall, this is a key area for you to discuss with your research support/finance colleagues because they will be best placed to take into account the various issues that affect the costing of research staff because there may be different approaches for each staff type. For example, a large grant might require you to include a full-time project manager and possibly other administrative support staff. The type of staff who may be costed into an application may include: the applicant (Principal Investigator or PI), postdoctoral research staff, technicians, administrative staff, project manager, and other researchers.

Operating costs

After you have considered your staffing costs, you will also need to think about the non-staff costs. These are all the other costs associated with running your project including the cost of consumables, equipment, travel and subsistence costs as well as the cost of accessing facilities, if required. Information Box 6.4 describes the type of costs you would need to include as part of your operating costs. We have included some examples to give you an idea of what to consider in your proposal.

Information Box 6.4

Types of operating costs

Type of Cost	Description	Examples
Consumables and small items of equipment	These relate to the purchase of (relatively) small items that are needed for and essential to the conduct of the project. For example, the UK Research Councils currently regard any equipment costing less than £10,000 (including VAT) as a consumable (part of the 'other directly incurred cost' on the application form. Other funders like the Leverhulme Trust in the UK have a different approach as they will not allow items of equipment that cost more than £1,000.	• laboratory consumables (e.g. pipettes, reagents, solvents) • data sets • computers/laptops including all the peripherals • software • data storage (e.g. IT servers) • recording devices
Larger items of equipment	These are formally regarded as equipment (rather than part of 'other directly incurred costs') and the funder may require you to provide quotations and even a business case for very high cost items. You will again need to work closely with your research support/finance team to make sure that your equipment items are costed and presented correctly.	• laser equipment

(Continued)

Type of Cost	Description	Examples
Other equipment costs	After obtaining the cost of purchasing the equipment itself you will also need to consider the other costs associated with such a purchase.	• relocation/installation • any modifications to the location of the equipment • maintenance/warranties • spares • software • import duty / VAT
Travel and subsistence	Projects frequently incur travel and subsistence costs, whether for yourself as the applicant, other academic colleagues or for your staff. Indeed, some schemes such as the Royal Society's International Exchanges Scheme are substantially geared towards travel and subsistence activities. As with other categories of cost the key issue is that the travel and subsistence costs must be justified and necessary for the project. It is worthwhile discussing your plans for travel with your colleagues in the research support/finance team as they might be able to provide some indicative costs and consider other issues – for example, using rates for mileage, meals, and so on, that are based on your employer's policies.	• journeys that are essential for the conduct of the project, e.g. field work • meetings with academic and industrial partners • the cost of flights and other internal travel (trains/taxis/car hire) • accommodation costs and the cost of meals • visa costs • conferences whether in your own country, nearby countries or other overseas locations (for example, registration fees)
Other costs	Essentially these are any other costs that have not already been covered above! The 'other costs' are really entirely dependent on the nature of your project and the activities that you will need to undertake to achieve your project's aims.	• management of the project with advisory board meetings • hosting workshops (e.g. as part of your dissemination/impact/public engagement activities) • translation costs if working overseas • transcription costs for interviews • certain publication costs (NB UK Research Councils will not fund Open Access costs) • postage and printing costs • casual staff employed via an agency • participant payments and incentives for research involving volunteers • cost of questionnaires • interview costs • data storage costs

Type of Cost	Description	Examples
		• specialist books not available at the University and required for the project
		• survey costs
		• hire of vehicles
		• field work/fees
		• costs of Visiting Researchers
		• purchase of data sets
		• access to other organisations' facilities
Subcontracts	You might occasionally need to employ some specialist expertise on your project which is not available from either yourself, your fellow investigators or your employer. Again, the precise expertise required will depend entirely on the nature of your project. You will need to obtain formal quotations from the potential supplier, which are based on and refer to a specific array of work. You should work with your research support/finance team to identify any potential procurement issues (for example, the need to go out to **tender**). You may need to consider tax issues, for example, in the UK, VAT will need to be considered.	• accessing a specialist facility • working with a video production company
Facilities	You may need to access your employing University's facilities and the technical staff that help to run the facilities. Contact your Facilities Manager to discuss your project and to obtain a quotation for the cost of the access and use of their facilities. This may also raise further ideas for more consumables that you would need to purchase.	• specialist laboratories • microscopes
Overheads	Overheads are those costs which are associated with your project but not directly incurred by your project (sometimes called indirect costs) such as the cost of general support provided to your project by your Institution. This support is provided in many ways, and the Full Economic Costing (FEC) approach attempts to allocate a small proportion of such running costs to specific projects by looking at relevant staff time. Your research support/finance colleagues will be able to calculate the overhead to be allocated to your project.	• library use and staff • payroll and HR staff • research support and finance staff • provision of labs and office space • maintenance of buildings • insurance on premises • running costs of the utilities

(Continued)

Type of Cost	Description	Examples
Ineligible costs	It is very important to note that not all costs are eligible for funding. In fact, there is quite a wide variation in approach from funder to funder, and indeed from scheme to scheme, on whether particular costs will be funded either wholly, partially or not at all. Your research support/finance colleagues will help you identify the ineligible costs for your specific funder.	• UK Research Councils will fund the full economic cost including FEC overheads, but only usually at an 80% funding rate although some costs may be funded at only 50% or not allowed at all. • Charitable trusts usually will not fund the costs of permanent members of staff (for example, other academic colleagues) and they usually will not fund overheads. • The European Commission will fund eligible costs at 100% but will not fund FEC overheads. They will instead apply a 25% flat rate overhead to most types of direct cost.

When submitting your proposal, reviewers will look carefully at your proposed budget to confirm that your costings are realistic and that you will be able to achieve the aims and outcomes of your research within the requested budget. However, in some cases, the review panel may ask the PI to lower some costs before awarding the grant or they may decide to award the grant but for less than the requested amount. If this is the case, you will be asked to provide the funder with a revised and realistic budget, but you will need to ensure that this does not compromise the quality of your research and outcomes. Discussing the amendments with the funder, senior colleagues and the research office will be important.

Conclusions

Careful planning and presentation of a realistic budget for your research project in your funding application demonstrates an awareness of the realities of carrying out a research project, and thus will instil confidence in the reviewers and panel members assessing your full application. Seeking expert advice from colleagues and those who work in the research office or finance department of your institution is key to being successful in navigating this section of your application successfully.

Further reading

Visit the Vitae webpages (www.vitae.ac.uk/) and read the sections on *Applying for research funding*, especially the section on *Costing and pricing a research proposal*. Vitae is a non-profit programme, part of The Careers Research and Advisory Centre (CRAC) Ltd, which supports the professional development of researchers.

Denicolo, P. and Becker, L. (2012) *Success in Research: Developing Research Proposals*. London: Sage

7

Gathering and using feedback

In this chapter you will explore:

- What is meant by feedback
- Why it is important
- How to achieve useful feedback
- How to use feedback effectively

Introduction

Previous applicants all quote "getting feedback" as a key part of being success-ful in securing research funding. However, although this is widely accepted as a vital step in putting together a funding application, there is limited explora-tion of what feedback really means in this context. So, here we will discuss the important questions about feedback in relation to seeking funding for a research project.

First, what do we mean by feedback in this context? We would define feedback as *constructively critical responses from knowledgeable others on the value of your project proposal*, while the purpose of getting feedback on your application is to gather information about its potential for being funded. The feedback should consist of advice and comments that aim to increase that potential. This advice and the comments will address things such as: the case you present for the research need, the design of the proposed project, the argument for the value of the results, the fit with the funder (as discussed in Chapter 2), the clarity of the writing, and how well you have demonstrated that you meet the assessment criteria for the funder or sponsor. You can then use the feedback you receive to make changes designed to enhance these aspects and thereby increase the potential of your application being funded.

This demonstrates how important it is to get feedback on your application to increase your chances of being successful. We can use the Johari's window model to illustrate this further. While the name 'Johari's window' sounds exotic, the name is formed from an amalgamation of the names Joseph and Harry, which are the forenames of the American psychologists Joseph Luft and Harry Ingham. Luft and Ingham created the term 'Johari window' to describe their model of interpersonal awareness, which was first published in 1955 (Luft and Ingham, 1955), and was subsequently developed by Joseph Luft (Luft, 1969). All very interesting, but what does this have to do with feedback for your funding application? The best way to show this is to look at the visual model of Johari's window. As you can see in Figure 7.1, the model is a quadrant; the vertical axis relates to what is known by you, with self-disclosure allowing the open/freely available quadrant to expand. The horizontal axis relates to what is known by others, with feedback being the key to increasing to the open area.

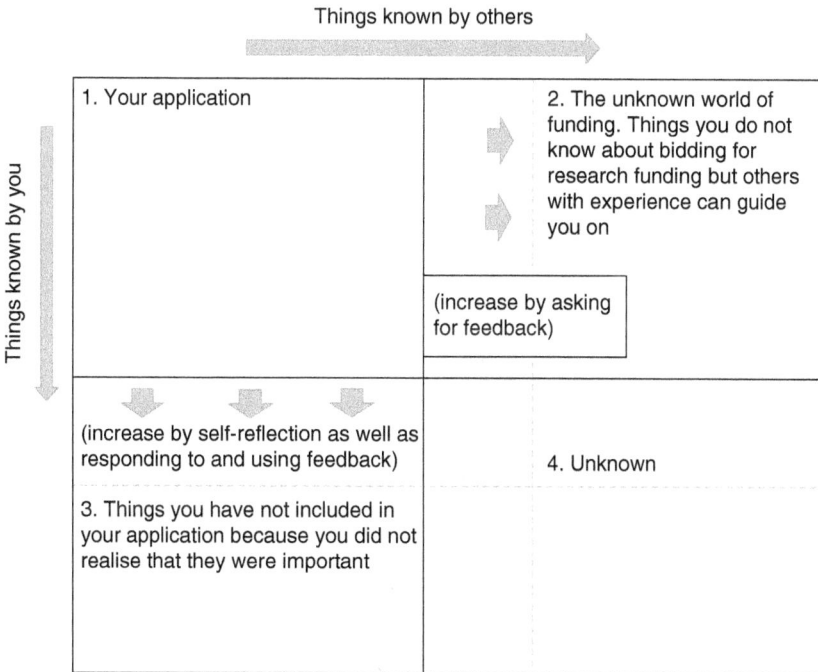

Figure 7.1 Version of Johari's window based on the work of Joseph Luft and Harry Ingham

The key to increasing your chances of success in a funding bid is to increase the exposure of your application (number 1 on the diagram) to include things known by others and thus decrease the size of the 'Unknown world of funding' or your blind spot, that is, what you are unaware of (number 2 on the diagram). Examples of this could be that you are unaware that you are using overly technical language in your lay person summary, or that you have not included enough detail in your justification of resources for conference attendance. To help reduce your 'unknown world' you will need to use the experience and wisdom of others (no one is born with the innate knowledge of the level of detail needed in a justification of resources section on a fellowship application!), and the mechanism to grasp this experience and wisdom is to **ask for feedback**. Similarly, there may be a host of experiences and evidence that you have mistakenly not included in the section on 'researcher track record' because you did not think that your experience as a member of the Health and Safety committee for the Department was relevant to a research proposal. These are things known by you that, once you realise that they are valuable, you can add to your application.

Asking for feedback and imposter syndrome

This all sounds sensible and fairly obvious; the problem lies with putting it into practice. You may think that is straightforward too, but for many researchers the issue of Imposter Syndrome invades this space and causes problems in seeking feedback. Imposter Syndrome is something that affects high achievers, often perfectionists, and is, therefore, rife in academia. You are, therefore, likely to suffer or to have suffered from this syndrome. Do not panic, it is not a medical condition, but a term used to describe patterns of behaviour and feelings in which the individual believes that everybody else is better/doing better/more intelligent/knows more than them/has written more eloquent book chapters (sorry, that is maybe just us), and s/he will be exposed as a fraud. Such people doubt their accomplishments and, despite evidence of their competence, for example in achieving a doctorate, securing a postdoc position through a rigorous recruitment process, publishing papers, or presenting at international conferences, they discount these as luck and they believe that they do not deserve what they have achieved. If we put this in the context of a funding bid application and Imposter Syndrome, it can be challenging to let someone else see your draft proposal and invite them to give you feedback. You will convince yourself that the reviewer will 'find you out' because you 'don't really know what you are doing', 'your research ideas are all rubbish anyway, and no one would fund this'. You could easily talk yourself out of giving it to anyone at all or you could hold on to it for a lot longer than necessary (or useful) to perfect your ideas, prose and grammar (perfectionist tendencies take over). Both these options are not helping with the aim of getting feedback, which we hope we have already convinced you is a vital step in this process. See Activity 7.1 for some ideas about overcoming Imposter Syndrome symptoms in the context of asking for feedback on your funding bid application.

Activity 7.1

Working on overcoming Imposter Syndrome when preparing a funding bid

- Acknowledge it exists and that you may have it.
- Share your concerns with a friend, peer or colleague.
- Get some coaching to help you through the process. This might be through a staff development or researcher development programme team.
- Find a mentor (either through a formal institutional scheme designed to help with your funding bid or through your own endeavours). Be honest with them about your concerns.
- Remember that most other applicants will have had such help and support and will use others' feedback to polish their bids. Do not disadvantage your chances by not doing so.
- Recognise that the disappointment of not getting the funding you sought would be enhanced by realising that you might have got it if only you had sought help as others did.

Having dealt with any feelings of Imposter Syndrome and having acknowledged that getting feedback is important, the next step is to ask for and obtain useful feedback. This might sound obvious but the key is to ask for and obtain *useful* feedback. As you may already be painfully aware, asking and obtaining useful feedback are not always straightforward so we will look at these issues, which are intimately entwined.

Getting useful feedback

The first thing to consider is what feedback would be useful to you at this specific phase in your application. You need to decide what you need help with and at what stage because, when it comes to seeking help, the most useful feedback is not likely to all come from one source. For example, the most useful feedback on the lay person summary may come from a different person to that on the methods and technical aspects of your application.

How to select reviewers for feedback ahead of submission

Once you have decided what feedback you need at different stages of your application, you will then need to select reviewers to ask for their help. You are likely to select them based on their expertise and experience. However, you should also factor in their availability and willingness to help within a certain timeframe. It is no use getting detailed and useful feedback an hour before the deadline when it is too late to do anything with it. As with many academic endeavours, giving feedback is usually done on a goodwill and favour basis. Thus, you may want to build up some 'credit' in that department through reciprocity: by helping with reviewing journal papers, reading drafts of student reports, helping with seminar series ... all good experiences for helping with grant writing too.

You will also need to consider how many different people to ask. As with all good research it is unwise to rely on one source. On the other hand, it may not be useful to receive 20 different opinions on one part of your application. Use Activity 7.2 to develop a plan for obtaining feedback.

Activity 7.2

What you need feedback on and who can provide it

Make a list of things to ask for feedback on and suggestions for who might be able to help. There are generic suggestions below but please consider *specifically* who would be able to help *you* with each of the following:

Section	Who could help?
Lay person or non-technical summary	There may be a research office or bid development team at your institution who can provide assistance with this section. Alternately, seek out someone who is not within your immediate research team or research area to provide comments. For a truly lay person perspective ask a family member, friend or administrator within your department who has no research experience.
Justification of resources	Check if your institution's Research Finance team can offer support with this section.
Impact summary and plans	A mentor with experience of writing and reviewing these sections
Case for support/ project outline	Peers and senior colleagues, collaborators. Your institution may have academic writing support available to help with communicating your ideas in the written word.
CV	Careers Advisors or Researcher Development teams may be able to offer support on this section. See also 'What every postdoc needs to know', Vitae website.

Section	Who could help?
Career and professional development	Seek advice from Researcher Development or Staff Development teams at your institution.
Interview	See Chapter 9

There may be institutional systems and processes for peer review or for mentoring researchers through funding applications. Consider, use and engage with these. In some institutions this is, in fact, compulsory to protect and enhance its research reputation and to increase the chances of research income being brought in. The processes they put in place are designed with this in mind. This overlaps with your desire to fund your specific research project so find out about these processes well ahead of your application deadline (see Chapter 3 on planning) to take full advantage of these opportunities.

Another group of people to consider seeking feedback from are those who have been successful in obtaining grants from that funder in the past. These can be found either from your Research Office, or equivalent, for people in this category in your own institution, or on the funder's website for external people. Especially for the latter you must factor in sufficient time for them to receive and respond to your carefully worded request for advice. They might even be generous enough to send you a copy of their proposal so that you can see what a successful application looks like.

Be specific in what you are asking for

Once you have a plan from whom to ask for feedback, the next thing is to be specific about the sort of feedback you are seeking. It can be very annoying to get feedback correcting your placement of commas when what you are really seeking is advice on the content, that is, whether you are on the right track with what has been included. The first step is to consider what feedback you would value: proof-reading, editing, substance or style. The second step is to be explicit in asking for this when you put in your request for help. Some reviewers, so indoctrinated into marking, may not be able to help correcting grammatical errors and typographical mistakes (some of you will be correcting grammatical errors whilst reading this!) but all efforts and help should be gratefully received with thanks. What you choose to do with the feedback you receive is up to you, but we will come to that later.

There will be a natural change in the type of feedback that is useful at different stages in the drafting of your application. If your reviewers are willing to re-read draft versions following your corrections and updates, the feedback should change from substance to style and then to editing and finally to proof-reading as your drafts progress towards the final version. For more ideas on how to access feedback and support, refer to Information Box 7.1.

Information Box 7.1

Alternate places and sources of feedback

Grant surgeries are a means for successful, unsuccessful and in-preparation bids from a department, school or faculty to be discussed and reviewed, and they are a great way to gain an insight into the world of research funding. These surgeries may be workshop-style sessions or online wiki pages (or similar). Check if these take place at your institution, or you could investigate the possibility of them being established. Learning from the mistakes or feedback received by others will help hone your own application and avoid the common pitfalls. Having your own application open to 'dissection' at a grant surgery event may be daunting but will likely provide comprehensive feedback whilst allowing others to learn from your experience too.

Reading advice and guidance documents produced by funders and sponsors. It is in the best interests of scheme and funding managers working for the funding agency to receive excellent applications that fit their remit and scheme criteria from which they can then choose which ones to fund. There are, therefore, often detailed and scheme-specific guidance documents that will include advice on what (and what not) to include in each section as well details of the assessment criteria and any general tips. Be especially careful with those bids that are submitted electronically because they are (mechanically) ruthless in cutting off any words beyond those allocated for specific boxes. If there is an allowance for X characters, check if these include spaces between words.

Talk to the scheme manager at the funding agency As with the point above, it is to the advantage of the funding agency to receive high-quality applications that fit their remit; therefore, scheme managers are generally happy to chat with researchers at an early stage of their bid preparation about whether the proposed research project (focus and approach, at least) fits within the criteria for specific funding streams.

Recommended blog posts and voices of experience. There are many webpages, blog posts and books which will offer advice, tips and voices of experience about funding. Please see the references and resources section at the end of this chapter for some that we recommend. The advice will be generic but nonetheless useful.

Workshops run by staff development teams, professional bodies or societies. Your institution may run workshops about preparing funding bids so investigate these, because they should be particularly useful for understanding local systems and processes. Professional bodies and societies may also run sessions as part of an annual conference or a development programme. For example, the Society for Research into Higher Education

(SRHE) runs a series of workshops throughout the year at its headquarters in London, and the British Society of Immunology congress ran a session aimed at early career researchers about funding to which representatives from major funders in this discipline were invited to speak.

Written or oral feedback

Feedback may come in different formats. What format it takes can influence the way the message is received. In oral communication the message is commonly reported as being only 7% about the words that are spoken with the remainder being related to the tone of voice and body language. In written feedback the elements of tone and humour can be lost and misinterpreted. However, both formats have pros and cons. Please see Information Box 7.2 for a comparison of written versus oral feedback before we discuss the art of receiving feedback.

Information Box 7.2

Comparison of written and oral feedback

Written	Oral
Considered and distilled	May be less concise and less ordered
Delay in seeking answers to questions where there is ambiguity or lack of clarity in the comments	Can ask immediate questions for clarification of any points raised
Risk of misinterpretation of tone of comments	Tone of comments can be more easily interpreted, unless there are cultural barriers/differences
Can take longer for the reviewer to produce	Can be quicker for the reviewer
Provides a record of the reviewer's comments	Can be harder for the recipient to retain all the relevant points, and relies on the recipient making notes accurately to reflect the points raised by the reviewer
Can be done at a time and place convenient for the reviewer, and read at a time and place convenient for the recipient	Relies on a face-to-face meeting (or video conference) – both parties need to be available at the same time

Being open to receiving feedback

Wherever your feedback comes from and in whatever format, you will need to be open to receiving it. This sounds obvious but you will need to be mindful of the fact that giving useful and straightforward feedback in a constructive way is a skill. Importantly, it is a skill that many people do not fully possess. Please remember this, both when you are giving and receiving feedback.

Here we will focus on receiving written feedback on your application, which is the most common form. Imagine the situation where you have just spent three weeks and sleepless nights working diligently and obsessively on a draft that you think is the best you can do. You are convinced that, while not perfect, it is a good first draft and there will only be a few changes needed. The feedback comes back from your senior and experienced colleague that your work needs major re-writing and re-thinking due to major flaws in the design of your work and the logical progression of your ideas. Receiving that feedback can be deflating and demoralising, and it may bring out your defensive side. You may want to argue your points.

As a contrast, consider an alternative scenario in this situation. What if the reviewer had skimmed through the application without really engaging with the content so only passed on a few minor suggestions for change? Your blind spot would not have been expanded (refer back to Johari window in Figure 7.1). Overall, you would be worse off. Although the pain of dealing with a major re-write or re-think might be more immediate, in the longer term it will serve you better. You may also want to consider this scenario when you are asked to give feedback to others. It is important to provide considered and honest feedback, or none at all; a half-hearted version may be more damaging than helpful since it will instil false confidence.

Even if you are open to feedback and understand that the feedback is in your own best interests, receiving the feedback in the scenario above will still be painful and you can justifiably feel upset. The best approach to deal with this (tried and tested by many, including authors writing this book) is to thank your reviewer and leave it for a short time (especially if you are feeling defensive or annoyed). Put it in a drawer or close your computer, then do something else. Preferably leave it until the next day or until you feel able to come back to it with an open mind. A skilled reviewer and mentor will be able to help you expand your potential by not just pointing out what is wrong or needs changing but by guiding you towards how to achieve the changes they believe are necessary.

For example, what is 'wrong' might be 'there is not enough detail in your section on plans for travel and dissemination'. A helpful and skilled reviewer would suggest how to tackle this; for example, 'Check where and when the next *International Symposium on Great Research in Your Particular Field* is happening so that you can include estimated costs to present your research at that event', or 'talk to Sam in Electrical Engineering who recently put together an application for a similar funding opportunity – they had a great section on travel and dissemination plans with some interesting public engagement ideas. Sam will be able to give you some ideas and advice specifically on this'. This happier situation is one to be hoped for and emulated, while less skilful ones just have to be tolerated but learnt from.

What to do with the feedback

In summary, you should: thank, leave, review, then decide what to do. The last point is important, 'decide what to do'. A useful analogy for feedback is to treat it as a gift. Some gifts are really useful and valuable to you, some gifts are lovely but are not actually needed; ultimately, they just clutter up your house, and some are not wanted or useful in any way. Useful and valuable in the context of feedback can mean positive or negative (negative meaning a criticism or a challenge). This means that some feedback may not be used; you do not need to use every suggestion that is given to you.

The decision about what to do with each piece of feedback should be influenced by first considering who is giving you the feedback and thinking about whose opinion holds the most value for each section of your application. This process can be useful when deciding how to proceed when you face the challenge of feedback from different sources contradicting each other, which is common for instance when receiving reviews from journals on submitted articles. You may also face the scenario of one reviewer suggesting changes to their own previous changes. This might be the time to get another opinion altogether. However, one specific kind of opinion to take notice of is those that suggest that they do not understand your point, or that indicate through comments that there is a misunderstanding. If one person is unclear, then the funder's reviewers might have a similar response.

Once you have decided what feedback to use, this will inevitably lead to re-drafting parts of your application and going through the process again (at *least* once). Applications are likely to go through many iterations before a final version is produced. This is usually a lengthy process but will result in the best possible written application you can produce, so is worth the effort. Do factor in such iterations of writing, gaining feedback and re-writing into the timescale for your funding bid preparation.

A note on feedback from funders

See Top Tip 7.1 for feedback from funders about the problems that reviewers and panel members commonly find in reading and assessing applications for research funding.

Top Tip 7.1

Feedback from funders

Your application should not:

- be written for specialists;
- include too much complex language and discipline-specific jargon;
- contain too many assumptions;
- have an unclear methodology/methods section leaving the reader to wonder how you will achieve your aims and objectives;
- be overly repetitive and include significant redundancy between sections;
- lead the reader to think that you have spent a long time crafting the case for support at the expense of other sections;
- bore the reader! The writing should be engaging and interest the reader from the first page;
- be structurally confusing;
- fail to address the 'So what?' of your research.

Consider the points in Top Tip 7.1 alongside the common reasons for rejection of proposals, which we will consider in more detail in the next chapter. In summary, the reasons for rejection of proposals are grouped into three areas: lack of consideration of the funder's remit and requirements; coherence, clarity and quality of the research proposal; investigator and/or composition of the research team. Whilst some factors included in these reasons will be outside of your control, a large proportion of these issues and mistakes can be avoided, especially the coherence and clarity of the full application. The style of writing for funding applications could be considered as a strange combination of academic writing, marketing and mainstream journalistic writing. The term **'grantsmanship'** is often used in reference in bid preparation and has been coined to specifically describe this unique style of writing. Grantsmanship describes the set of skills required, combined with the craft or art of preparing a research funding proposal (see Further reading for more on grantsmanship: Coley and Scheinberg, 2008).

Getting feedback will help you to gain an insight into the art of 'grantsmanship', and will help ensure that your proposal is both well-written and that it does not fall into any of the common traps for rejection. Therefore, obtaining and using feedback is a sensible and strategic step to help your application in its voyage towards successfully being funded.

Conclusion

In conclusion, obtaining and using useful feedback is cited by successful applicants as the most important factor in achieving research funding, and should be sought throughout and beyond the application stage. Such careful preparation takes time, which you should not underestimate. If you are as yet only contemplating bidding for funding or do not yet have a specific project in mind, take every opportunity to volunteer feedback to colleagues on their proposals or, indeed, seek opportunities to become a project reviewer for funders in your discipline. It is always easier to spot problems in others' work than in your own but, with practice, the latter becomes easier as you are alerted to issues that are important. You will then more readily don a critical reviewer's hat when reviewing your own work. What is more, you will become more sympathetic to the reviewers' viewpoints when you receive critical feedback yourself.

In the next part of the book we will look at the stages post-submission of your application.

References and further reading

British Society for Immunology webpages: www.immunology.org/
Carlson, M. and O'Neal-McElrath, T. (2008) *Winning Grants: Step by Step* (3rd ed.). San Francisco: Jossey-Bass
Coley, S. M. and Scheinberg, C. A. (2008) *Proposal Writing: Effective Grantsmanship* (3rd ed.). Thousand Oaks, CA: Sage
Elvidge, E., Spencely, C. and Williams, E. (2017) *What Every Postdoc Needs to Know*. World Scientific Publishing
Luft, J. and Ingham, H. (1955) *The Johari Window: A Graphic Model of Interpersonal Awareness*. Proceedings of the western training laboratory in group development. Los Angeles: UCLA
Luft, J. (1969) *Of Human Interaction: Johari Model*. Mayfield Publishing Company
Society for Research into Higher Education (SRHE) webpages: www.srhe.ac.uk/
Vitae webpages: www.vitae.ac.uk/

PART III

Post-application steps and future planning

8

The assessment processes

In this chapter you will engage with:

- Who the reviewers are likely to be
- The stages of the assessment process
- How research funders make decisions
- How to respond to reviewers' feedback

Introduction

Funders cannot fund all the proposals they receive, so they have implemented rigorous assessment processes to ensure scientific rigour, strategic fit and support for research that is of the highest quality. This process is aimed at being robust, transparent, fair and is informed by high-calibre researchers who will help the funders make the best decision possible. Understanding this process will help you to write better and more successful research proposals.

In previous chapters, we have discussed the key stages of the application process and how to put together a research proposal. In this chapter, we would like you to consider the stages of assessment your application is likely to go through and how you can influence these steps despite the impression that they seem to be more controlled by the funder than the researcher. Here you will learn about the things that you can do at the application stage that will help you increase your chances of success.

The stages of the assessment process

Generally speaking, funders follow a two-stage process to review applications: processing and screening your application followed by a peer-review process. The first stage is primarily conducted by the funder and the second stage involves selected experts in the field. Even though some funders may add other steps to the peer-review process, these two broad stages are common to most of them.

Processing and screening your application

The office responsible for managing the programme or funding scheme you applied to will process your application before sending it for scientific peer review. Usually, an internal committee carries out a first screening to confirm that you meet the eligibility criteria (e.g. discipline, number of years after PhD or as a post-doctoral researcher, country) and that your proposal adheres to the guidelines provided. Even though this process may slightly vary across funders, all of them will make sure that the research proposal is within their remit and that all the required information has been provided and formatted in accordance with their guidelines (e.g. number of pages, font size, margins).

To avoid disappointment, it is good practice to allow yourself enough time to go through the full application before submitting it as most funders will return your proposal at this stage if you have missed any information or the application does not comply with their criteria. Start the process as early as possible to meet the closing date with all checks completed.

Peer-review process

Peer review at this stage comprises two steps aimed at helping the funder make a transparent and fair decision although this process may vary slightly from funder to funder and funding scheme: independent (external) peer review followed by an internal assessment panel. However, in some cases, the independent reviewers may also be members of the assessment panel and take part in the overall review process. It is important that you familiarise with the review process and assessment criteria of your selected funder because this will help you both to know who the reviewers are and anticipate what they will be looking for in your application.

Independent peer review

After the first screening, all proposals that are deemed suitable are sent, in confidence, to three or more independent expert peer reviewers (national and international) who are working in the relevant research area. When recruiting reviewers, research funders look for individuals who are leading experts in their field and who have reached a reputable standing within the research community. Reviewers come from different areas and backgrounds, but significantly they understand about quality in research in several areas and beyond their specialist area. Experts come from different sectors such as academia, research institutes, industry, government, international agencies, and the public in general. In addition, reviewers respect and practise a number of core peer-review principles such as integrity, fairness, transparency, confidentiality and impartiality.

As a general rule, funders ask the reviewers or referees to consider a number of core criteria and to use a specific scoring system when assessing the proposals that they are allocated. The reviewers' scores and their comments will be the basis for discussion at the internal assessment panel. Information Box 8.1 describes the most common criteria used during the peer-review process (we provide a more detailed checklist later in the chapter), but we strongly recommend that you identify and clearly address those relevant to your specific funder to increase your chances of success. You can find them either in the application guidelines or on their website.

Information Box 8.1

Core assessment criteria

- **Excellent and innovative science**. This is a key criterion and all proposals, irrespective of the field and the funding scheme, must be of high quality (refer to Chapter 5 for more details on how to write your proposal). Peer reviewers will consider the originality, importance and scientific potential of the proposal, the relevance of the research question and whether the research proposed will reduce current knowledge gaps and broaden our understanding of the field. They will check that the methodology and the general plan are feasible and good enough to help you achieve your aims and objectives.
- **Bringing together the right research team and in the best research environment**. Funders want to be reassured that the researcher/s involved in the proposal are capable of conducting the proposed research well. Reviewers will look at and provide comments on the research area, skills and experience of the investigator(s)

(Continued)

and the team (if applicable) to deliver the proposed research. They will also check track records of all team members relative to their career stage, their expertise and contribution to the research. Several funders value the contribution that multidisciplinary teams bring to the proposal and may require the applicant to include relevant disciplines in the application.

- **Timeliness**. This refers to the extent that the proposal is topical and currently relevant and whether it will bring future benefits at national and international levels.
- **Value for money**. Funders pay specific attention to the resources requested in any application and they will ask reviewers to assess the extent to which the scientific potential and importance of the research question justify the amount of funding that has been requested in the application. Your finance department and other colleagues at your Institution are familiar with these requirements and they can provide you with expert advice on how to address this criterion in your application. Chapter 6 describes in more detail the financial aspects that need to be considered when preparing a funding application.
- **Societal and economic impact**. Most funders may also assess the benefits that your research will bring to society and the economy and the plans you have included to achieve this impact. We recommend that you carefully think about the potential impact of your proposal and how you will achieve it after the completion of your research project. In Chapter 5 you will find a longer description of what impact means and how to address it in your proposal.

Knowing and understanding the funders' assessment criteria will help you to anticipate what the reviewers are expecting to see in your application. Careful attention to this at the application stage enhances your chances of success.

Internal assessment panel

Having passed through the independent reviewer filter process, depending on the funder and type of scheme, the applications will then be considered for discussion by some form of internal panel. There could be one single assessment panel or several panels, each one reviewing proposals within their specialist areas. For instance, the Medical Research Council (MRC) from UK Research and Innovation (UKRI), has about 12 expert panels, each one covering one scientific area.

Members of this panel are all experts in the general, but probably not all in the specific field, and they do not re-review the proposals again, rather they prioritise them and make comments on the quality of the proposal and the potential to receive funding. If the proposal is deemed not to be competitive, it will be rejected, and the applicant will be informed about their decision. Some funders send anonymous feedback to applicants, which undoubtedly is very useful to improve the quality of future applications.

When making decisions, the panel considers the scores and comments from the independent reviewers, the evaluation criteria and the applicants' response (if applicable – see Chapter 9). They reflect on the scores and feedback received for each application and the chair of the panel asks other members to actively contribute to the discussion before any final decision is made. We provide examples of specific review processes next.

For instance, the Volkswagen Foundation in Germany conducts an initial checking to verify whether their requirements have been addressed in the applications. If eligible, the proposals are sent for external review. Depending on the funding scheme, the Foundation can request written expert opinions (usually three per application), or send the proposals to an expert committee, or a combination of the two. Based on recommendations of the reviewers, the Board of Trustees or the Secretary General make a final decision.

The National Institute for Health (NIH, USA) uses several scientific review groups (or study sections) to assess research proposals relevant to their scientific expertise. When assessing proposals, members of these groups are assigned pre-meeting activities such as writing their feedback and scoring the application based on NIH's criteria. In contrast to what we described above, NIH also asks the reviewers to take part in the panel meeting and contribute to final funding decisions. Reviewers are also asked to consider several criteria such as the overall impact of the proposed research, significance, innovation, track record of the principal investigator and the team/collaborators, research environment, training potential (if applicable) and possibilities of technology transfer (if applicable).

Some funders, a diminishing number in economically stretched climates, give some applicants the opportunity to respond to reviewers' comments when their proposal is deemed potentially fundable although it raised a few questions. They request applicants to respond in writing to clarify some aspects of the proposal before they make a final decision. The applicant is given a deadline and, when the required information has been returned, the proposal is assessed within the internal panel alongside the written response and any other information available. This is a positive sign that your proposal might be considered for funding and your response becomes a very important step in the application process.

Re-submission

As we indicated, once an application has been rejected most funding organisations do not allow re-submission and even those that do will expect you to take account in detail of assessors' comments, maintaining all the many things they surely held as exceptionally good while taking account of the small but important issues they highlight for review.

Benefiting from the feedback

Responding to reviewers' comments is not a trivial step and a well-crafted response can increase your chances of getting funded (or not). If you search the internet you will find a few tips on how to respond to reviewers' feedback but, here, we give you some advice drawn from reviewers and funders themselves. It is also recommended that you discuss this great opportunity with other colleagues, particularly those who have been successful or, if possible, who take part in review panels.

A good response considers all points made and looks at comments in a positive way. The feedback received is not addressed to you personally but what the reviewers have understood from your proposal. You will recognise that much of what was said in Chapter 7 in relation to the feedback you seek before submission is relevant for post-submission feedback. However, below we summarise a few points that need to be considered when responding to post-submission, peer-review comments:

- **Do not take it personally!** Embrace their comments and get ready to give your best possible response. The reviewers do not know you and they are offering you another opportunity to be successful.
- **Understand the reviewers** and think about who will read your response. They are busy people and do not want to spend much time reading (or understanding) your proposal, the feedback received and your response.
- **Read the feedback more than once**; discuss with other colleagues who can help you in this part of the process. Read your proposal again to understand their comments better.
- **Be respectful and thank the reviewers**; be open to feedback and use a positive tone. Your response will reflect your attitude.
- **Be honest** and recognise any limitations that have been highlighted by the reviewers.
- **Address all comments raised by the reviewers** and make your response as simple as possible. Provide an explanation and reassure the panel that you have considered all their comments.
- **Do not repeat yourself**, explaining things in a different way. Use this opportunity to elaborate more on your proposal and, if necessary, add new information to make your point stronger.
- **Be concise and clear**, only including information that adds value to the point you are trying to make. Group together comments that refer to the same topic and provide a clear argument.

- **Make it easy for the reviewer to find your response in your proposal** by using the reference number provided (if any), or by identifying the relevant page and line numbers in your response, or by using a different font for insertions. Check with your funder whether there are any specific guidelines or preferences for how to present your response.
- **Stick to the formatting guidelines** provided by the funder. They may return your response if you fail to do this.

Whilst responding to feedback comments is not an easy task, this is a good opportunity to show that you really care about the funders' needs, that you are the right candidate and that you will do what you have promised to do in your proposal.

Responding to reviewers' comments after rejection

On first opening a rejection letter it is normal to feel grave disappointment, even anger at yourself and others although you already knew that the success rate is very low. You may well have cognitively prepared for such an eventuality, but our emotions are not so readily contained. It is sensible to put the letter in a drawer for a few days until you feel less emotional about it, have got used to the idea and can adopt a more measured perspective, recognising that this is not a reflection on you personally but is the result of a highly competitive situation. It is then worth reflecting on any weaknesses identified in your proposal, discussing them with others and considering how to avoid such issues in future. Make it a learning experience. Indeed, if you receive no feedback with a rejection, it is valuable to ask if some might be forthcoming to encourage your further development.

If most of the original feedback was highly positive except for issues that you can deal with effectively, you might ponder whether it might be worth applying elsewhere. If you do go down that route, resist simply sending the original proposal with those changes made. First check the guidelines and strategic priorities of the next potential funder to ensure that you orientate the proposal to their needs and requirements, paying attention to any guidance they give on structural requirements such as order and word length of sections. Also ensure that you reflect the language and vocabulary they use in calls for proposals. This is as important for success in a re-submission as it is for your first foray.

Reasons for award or rejection

In previous chapters, we have emphasised that research funding is highly competitive and that you need to prepare well in advance of the submission deadline.

We hope that with the information provided in this book you are more aware now that the ability to produce a fundable proposal depends on several factors. The main reason why anyone has success in a funding application is because they have met all the criteria required by the funder, which are likely to be a combination of many of those that we list as a checklist in Information Box 8.2.

We have provided there as many potential criteria that we can think of because each funding organisation has its own strategic priorities and, therefore, preferred criteria. For each proposal you submit, be sure to check those priorities when preparing your bid. You might like to check your draft proposal against our criteria below before finalising it and be prepared to answer questions based on these criteria in any interview.

Information Box 8.2

Checklist of criteria for judging proposals

- The topic aligns well with strategic priorities and is timely.
- The rationale is well argued, being clear, cogent and convincing.
- It draws on evidence from carefully selected, salient literature.
- It demonstrates that the research is germane to current concerns and is important.
- The research approach is rational and logically related to the topic.
- The design is clearly organised, making good use of the skills and resources available, including time.
- The techniques and instruments are described in detail and are appropriate for the type of data sought.
- There is evidence of creativity in the approach and design.
- The management of the process shows evidence of thoughtful planning.
- There is an evaluation strategy in place.
- The personnel included are well qualified for the tasks allotted.
- Ethics, Legal, Health and Safety issues have been carefully considered and built in to the project.
- Appropriate evaluation of progress during and at the end of the project has been included.
- The research environment/proposed institution is well regarded and supportive of the proposal.
- The budget is detailed and cost-effective.
- Issues of cultural sensitivity have been addressed.
- Enthusiastic and supportive references have been provided by esteemed scholars/researchers.
- The Principal Investigator has the requisite qualifications.
- The Principal Investigator provided evidence of commitment, versatility and leadership skills.
- The research team has been well selected to include the requisite range of expertise.

- The results should provide value for money and produce a measurable, positive impact.
- The dissemination of results and potential outcomes has been planned, targeting an appropriate audience of theorists, policy-makers and users.

Some of the most common reasons for rejection can be grouped into three categories, as presented below, and although we have discussed these across the different chapters in the book, we summarise them here for you.

Lack of consideration of the funder's remit and requirements

Several applications are rejected at the screening stage because they did not comply with the funder's requirement. It may be that the research area or topic presented is not within the funder's remit or that the applicants failed to read carefully and familiarise themselves with the guidelines so that the content, length and formatting of the proposal is not in line with their requirements. Do read all the information provided by the funder more than once and contact them if you have questions about your proposal and the funder's aims; talk to your research office (if available) and to more senior researchers who have experience with the funder or who have expertise in your field. This will save you time if you realise that it is not the right funder for you; it is also an excellent learning opportunity to understand the research funding process.

Coherence, clarity and quality of the research proposal

Some researchers may have a great scientific idea, but if they fail to demonstrate it in the proposal in a clear, innovative and convincing manner, it may be rejected. The proposal must be ambitious but not too risky; coherent and neat from start to end; and it must present a consistent and compelling story throughout the whole application. The abstract and lay summary are critical to your application since they are the first point of contact with the reviewer; both should be clear and understandable, demonstrating the significance and uniqueness of your research (see Voice of Experience 5.1).

Often, proposals that are rejected are poorly written, diffuse, and their lack of clarity does not allow the reviewer to understand and appreciate the research study. Proposals that contain an unreasonable number of mistakes reflect carelessness and lack of attention to detail. This is not acceptable to reviewers as the researcher may have the same attitude towards the development and completion of the study.

Unsuccessful applications may contain research questions, design and methods that are rather traditional, or that are unsuited to achieve the purpose and aims of the study. Reviewers may not find anything that strikes them as being innovative, or that will produce useful and original knowledge. Often, the objectives and stages of the research proposed are heavily related to one another so that the completion of the research might be compromised if the first stages are not accomplished.

Other aspects that may contribute to rejection are those associated with unrealistic budgets in terms of staff, equipment, assistantship and infrastructure; or costs may be too high for the proposed research. In some cases, the funders may ask the researcher to review the costings if the proposal is deemed fundable, but it is best to get it right the first time. Remember, though, that underestimating costs is as likely to merit rejection, because of risks to completion, as overestimating them.

In addition to addressing all points above, successful proposals provide enough preliminary evidence that strengthens their argument about the need to conduct research in that specific topic. The researchers strongly demonstrate that they know what they are talking about and, while there could be other ways of investigating the problem, their research design is advantageous and is thus the best approach.

A good way of overcoming the pitfalls listed above is to read the funder's materials, carefully think about your proposal, have it peer reviewed within your institution or colleagues, and address all comments received before submission. Colleague-reviewers at this stage (see previous chapter) will be able to identify any inconsistencies or problems with your proposal and they will ask questions that you may have not thought about. Their feedback will help you to produce a much stronger application.

The investigator and/or composition of the research team

Funding agencies and reviewers want to be reassured that the investigator and the research team can deliver the proposed research and that they will get value for money. Applications are likely to be unsuccessful if the Principal Investigator does not have adequate experience, seems unfamiliar to the field, has a track record that is not at the required level for the proposed research or they did not involve the right team for the project. It may well be that the researcher and the team can achieve the aims of the proposal, but they have not been able to demonstrate that in the proposal convincingly to the funder's panel.

To be competitive you need to catch the attention of the funder and the reviewers in positive ways rather than raising concerns, no matter that they may be niggling rather than serious ones.

Nevertheless, not all rejections are the result of poorly crafted proposals. There are some slightly more positive, palatable reasons for rejection as we describe next in Information Box 8.3.

Information Box 8.3

Some other possible reasons for rejection

If you have met all the submission deadlines and have obeyed all guidance from the funders on structural format, some possible reasons for your lack of success this time might be:

- The funder may have received several outstanding proposals on the same topic but only have enough financial capacity for one; yours was not selected but could have been.
- The funder's research strategic priorities may have changed since they were last published, perhaps because of government policy or a downturn in the general economy or some unexpected, critical occurrence.
- The cost of the project may exceed, from the funder's viewpoint, the benefits of the results, though you might have judged otherwise.
- There may have been a paradigm clash with influential members of the panel so that they would prefer a different approach and methods.
- It is perceived that industry/your institution/other funders should be funding it instead.

There is not much you can do to avert those kinds of problems, but you can deal with negative outcomes in a mature and proactive way, at least after safely venting your frustration at the unfairness of it all.

The stages at which rejection decisions can be made are clarified in the Voice of Experience 8.1, which concludes with an example that emphasises the point we made about the key importance of checking the funder's guidelines before submitting your proposal.

Voice of Experience 8.1

Filter stages and how to be rewarded

Assessing applications for funding as a charity trustee I have reflected on how we as funders select the candidates for our money. Thinking about my small experience of trying to get funding for educational research it seems to me that the process in both areas is like a series of filters that only catch part of the flow.

(Continued)

The first selection happens when the funders first look at the application. Many may go straight in the bin and never reach the next stage because they have failed to apply for the specified categories or are just totally unfocussed. At the next stage the grants team and committee look at the specifics of the suggested project, checking whether the description is clear and the timeframe and funding appropriate. Applications often fail to pass through this filter because they are not transparent about how the project funding will be managed or where they intend to get any additional finance they may need. Once safely through this filter, a member of the charity is sent to have a look and report back on how the proposed project looks on the ground when they meet those running it. If that's OK, the projects that are left then reach the main committee stage where they are usually agreed, and the sum adjusted. What the charity is looking for is clearly spelled out and, therefore, those who carefully read the brief do best.

Although these appear to be self-evidently sensible checks and filters when you are in the position of being a reviewer, they may not seem so obvious when you are applying for funding as a researcher. The funder's reviewers know what they are looking for and what they consider to be important questions. Prospective researchers need to find those things out as best they can, using the guidance provided and their own resources.

This reminds me of an incident at the start of my own research. I was observing a nursery teacher with her class gathered in front of her at the start of the day.

The days of the week were her focus for this stage and so she asks: 'What day is it today?' and the answer comes back 'Tuesday'.

'What does Tuesday start with?' she asks scanning the eager faces and chooses Tommy at the back.

'Getting up', he says firmly.

Not the answer she wants at all! She points at the days of the week chart to the first letter of the word Tuesday.

'T', says Tommy.

'Big T or little T?'

'Big T', says Tommy.

'Well done!'

Teachers always reward the answer they want! This teacher had in her mind which words should start with a capital letter.

What does your funder want?

Emeritus Professor

In conclusion, the assessment process is aimed at ensuring scientific rigour and high-quality research. Knowing and understanding it will help you anticipate what the reviewers are expecting to see in your application. Any feedback received will also help you write better and stronger proposals.

Further reading

Kenway, J., Boden, R. and Epstein, D. (2007) *Winning and Managing Research Funding: The Academic's Support Kit.* London: Sage

Marsh, H. W. and Ball, S. (1991) Reflections on the peer review process. *Behavioural and Brain Sciences*, 14: 157–8

Marsh, H. W., Jayasinghe, U. W. and Bond, N. (2008) Improving the peer review process for grant applications. *American Psychologist*, April: 160–8

9

Further steps in the application process: interviews

This chapter introduces you to:

- Variable pathways to the final decision
- Responding to feedback before the panel meeting
- The nature of interviews
- How to prepare well for interviews
- Managing the process: first impressions, body language and controlling nerves
- Receiving and reacting to the outcome

Introduction

After all the effort of preparing, checking and sending off your proposal it may seem like a good time to relax while awaiting the final decision. Certainly, a short break may support your general wellbeing, but there may be other aspects of the review process to prepare for. They form the substance of this chapter, while we also offer in the final section some advice about maintaining momentum. First though, it would be worthwhile checking the funder's documents and website about the flow path of their decision process which can range over variants of the following steps.

The decision may be made:

- entirely on your submitted proposal documents;
- after receiving your responses to reviewers' comments on your proposal;
- following a two-stage process that involves short-listing and interviews, which might include a presentation.

For the first case, the challenge is to maintain your enthusiasm for research in general and this proposed research specifically while sensibly preparing for both success and disappointment. For the second case, take heart and be proactive even though some of the feedback is likely to be annoying: they may seem to have misunderstood or underestimated some main points. As we said in the previous chapter, you should see this as an opportunity to clarify those aspects and add strength to your original propositions. It is important that you do respond, and respond in a positive, courteous, carefully constructed way (no matter how irritating you find the critique or questions raised). Although there will be a restriction on the number of words you can use to defend your case, this does provide you with an opportunity to elaborate on your original by thanking the reviewers for their 'insightful' or 'instructive' feedback then addressing their points succinctly.

The third option above, although a reason for some muted celebration, is more complex and forms the substance of the rest of this chapter, beginning with the purposes of interviews.

Interviews – when, why and sources of support

Interviews tend to be part of the processes for allocating very large awards or for personal fellowships or for awards provided by professional societies. In each case, the purpose is to assure the funders that from a small range of potentially excellent projects they can select the most effective one for their purposes, led by an applicant with the most promising potential. Therefore, while you should be delighted that you have been short-listed, demonstrating that on paper you look like a researcher with capability, credibility and high motivation, you need to prepare well to stand out and be successful in a group of similar high-flyers.

An early part of that preparation (indeed you could be thinking about this soon after submitting the documents while awaiting the first decision) is to gather together a list of all the resources of support available, those people who provided you with feedback on your draft proposals and others who provide a wider set of critical friends. This list will include those people with one of a variety of titles whose job it is to support funding applications, either centrally based or within Schools or Faculties, and who therefore know the requirements and foibles of funders as well as people who have been successful in their applications or have been panel members. These research support staff and those experienced others would be valuable helpers to suggest likely interview questions and provide mock interviews.

Further, you should recruit as many people as possible (with a wide variety of backgrounds from experts in your topic through to academics in the general field of it and current or previous fund or fellowship holders, to lay persons [friends and family]), to read your proposal and question you about it. In that way you can be alerted to strengths and weaknesses related to the theoretical, practical, methodological and budgetary aspects of the research as well as what is interesting about it and, critically, what can be misconstrued or is unclear. These are all potential sources of questions that might be used by the interview panel.

It can be quite a task and, therefore, a 'big ask' to read the whole proposal, so think about breaking it into sections for which each group might provide relevant expert questions. For instance, fellow researchers in your discipline might usefully challenge you about your literature review, any in your wider faculty could field questions on methodology, while friends outside the university could quiz you on the lay person's summary.

You should also think about the practicalities – the logistics of attending the interview.

Interviews – panels and topics

Having received your interview invitation, you can usefully make contact with one of the funder's administrators to confirm and/or clarify details about the interview such as expected length, whether or not a presentation will be expected, how long you will have and what facilities are available and allowed (such as PowerPoint, visual aids), the size and likely nature of the interviewing panel.

Interview panels

Panels can vary from three to around 15 people, with at least one senior person and one expert in the field, though they may be one and the same person. Knowing that the prospective panel is quite large, and likely to be seated around a large boardroom table, can help you prepare any presentation and gain practice responding to large groups rather than the more intimate discussion about you and your previous and proposed research that could occur with a small group. Obviously, you should not contact any potential panel members but if you can find out who they are likely to be, perhaps the funder's website lists experts from which panels are drawn, then you can research their interests and expertise to help you formulate possible questions and suitable responses.

There will be a chairperson who will perform introductions, manage the interview and chair the decision panel later. It is likely that it will have been decided in advance who will ask which questions and in which order, possibly with two or three lead questioners knowledgeable about some aspect of the research (theory, methodology, requirements of the funders) and perhaps others who may be asked to explore your personal approach to research, now and in the future, or aspects of your proposed research venue/institution.

You

Even the most assiduously designed research can falter if not managed by a competent person who does not panic when things fail to go to plan. Thus, funders must ascertain if you are that kind of person. They will seek evidence from your track record, such as publications, and measures of esteem achieved, promotions, invitations to give talks, or accolades won. They will want to be convinced of your developing independence as a researcher, in terms of decisions taken and problems solved. If your project involves you in working with others or leading a team, they will probably want to explore examples of your teamworking and leadership experience (either in or outside a research context) and may challenge you to consider how you might deal with specified problems, perhaps by using case scenarios.

Often questions emerge about how you view previous achievements and what your vision for the future is, in terms of the research focus and/or your own personal development. You will need to convince them that you are both dedicated and flexible, skilled but ready to learn, ambitious but realistic, confident but not arrogant. See the section on questions and answers below, but you can begin your advance preparation for any interview about your research by undertaking Activity 9.1.

Activity 9.1

Marketing yourself

While most of us in the academy can manage to include in our curriculum vitae such things as 'evidence of esteem', many of us find it difficult to 'sell ourselves' in face-to-face situations. We either feel we are being immodest, or showing off, or not bold enough, too diffident about our positive attributes or afraid of coming across as conceited and egotistical. To prepare to overcome these attitudes/beliefs is sensible because you must convince the panel that you are indeed the right person for the task.

(Continued)

You can start by looking at your CV, selecting parts that provide evidence of your most positive research attributes, such as those we listed in the first paragraph of this section (publications, measures of esteem, leadership, and so on). Then prepare a personal introduction or statement that truthfully but succinctly describes:

- your qualifications, and how they are relevant to the research you do;
- your key strengths, with examples of how you have demonstrated them;
- your research passions and how they have influenced the proposal (or any research you would like to pursue if you have not yet submitted a proposal);
- how colleagues view you and how you know this;
- a recent achievement relevant to your research;
- a challenge you met in previous research and how you successfully met it.

You then need to practise delivering such a statement – perhaps first alone, in front of a mirror, and then to a caring but honest friend for feedback on how trustworthy, confident but appropriately unpretentious you appear, as well as how convincing you are that you are enthusiastic about the project and that you are an exciting, highly competent researcher (whatever your discipline and context).

Place/research location

The situation in which your research will take place is also critical for its success. You will be required to justify that it is the best or most appropriate. The kinds of attributes of the location that will interest the panel are the availability of resources, such as equipment, facilities, adjunct expertise and complementary knowledge; the potential for collaboration; the support of senior colleagues and availability of professional development opportunities. It is likely that you have summarised these in your project proposal, but this may be the time to elaborate not only on what makes your venue specifically valuable for the success of the project, but how you investigated it to ensure its suitability. It is likely that in the proposal you described the venue succinctly so the interview may give you an opportunity to elaborate on its special suitability by giving examples of its research culture and facilities.

Project

As well as checking your proposal for aspects that may not be as clear as they could be or are liable to misinterpretation by the uninitiated, you should be able to convince the panel that the project is:

- important, timely and viable;
- based on a careful review of previous research;

- seeking to achieve realistic objectives through a carefully prepared plan;
- methodologically sound;
- using the skills and resources available;
- good value;
- distinctive and likely to have a significant impact in one realm, but preferably more than one, from: theoretical, social, economic, policy, environmental, cultural or health.

To do that you should be able to provide relevant examples and a robust defence of your choices, demonstrating that you are aware of alternatives but have a rationale for your final selections, and have a well-considered timeline, with key steps and deliverables. You should also be able to show that risks have been assessed and that you have prepared contingency plans in case of problems. It is realistic to recognise that most research encounters difficulties of some kind; the panel will want to be reassured that you can handle them to go on to complete the project.

If there has been a delay of several weeks or more between proposal submission and interview you might think about what developments have taken place in the field and what preliminary data you may have collected that might influence the project and what was proposed. You should prepare a cogent synopsis of intended successful outcomes of the project to convince experts and lay people about both its relevance and how it will contribute to your skills and career development (this especially if applying for fellowships of any kind).

Importantly, you should be prepared to demonstrate ownership of the project, no matter how many people helped you prepare the proposal, so it is well worth multiple readings of it before the interview so that you are familiar with every nuance. And yet, despite that familiarity you also need to show great enthusiasm, remembering how exciting the ideas seemed as you began preparing it. It is crucial that you infect the panel with your eagerness to engage in it and complete it satisfactorily.

Everything we have noted so far has led to the recommendation at the beginning of this chapter that you prepare well for interviews, practising and, wherever and whenever possible, requesting peers, colleagues and experts to engage you in robust questioning. In the next section we will explore the interview process further so that your practice can be made as realistic as possible.

Interview process

Every funding body has its own preferred format for the interview process, yet we can identify some recurrent aspects that you can prepare for in advance to impress the panel. The first issue we address is the need for you to manage the process. Yes, though the panel chair will technically be managing the process engaged in by the panel, you can manage your contribution to it. You can prepare for the actual day by ensuring that you have copies of all relevant documents, any presentation on a USB memory stick (with a paper copy just in case), any hand-outs you might like to distribute and a sensible travel plan that allows for delays. Let us start with your punctual arrival.

Managing the process

First impressions

Not only is punctuality important but you must also consider your appearance, because people tend to make important judgements about others within the first few seconds of meeting. This is an important occasion, so your appearance should reveal you as an aspirational researcher who is smart and business-like. When you enter the room, offer a smile to the whole panel, make eye contact with each one briefly and offer a firm handshake or other greeting that is culturally appropriate to individuals. While they should be making efforts to put you at ease, you can reciprocate, taking your attention away from how *you* feel to how *they* must feel. It is probable that they will be desperate to make a good decision for the organisation while, at the same time, wanting to encourage you to present yourself in the best light.

Ice-breakers

Of course, seasoned panel members will recognise that anyone would be nervous in such a situation: there are few people who enjoy being interviewed. Therefore, there is likely to be some form of ice-breaker, something to allow you to relax a little before the serious interrogation begins. This is often in the form of an introduction to the panel with thanks for your attendance and a suggestion that you introduce yourself to them. This is where your practice at marketing yourself in Activity 9.1 comes in useful. Alternatively, they could ask you to rehearse key points of your proposal, a good reason to be thoroughly familiar with it and to have prepared a synopsis of especially interesting aspects for just such an eventu-ality. They might ask you for its USP – unique selling point. Be prepared to speak about that fluently.

It is not just what you say in presentations and interviews but how you say it that will be an important contributor to your success.

Body language

It is said that in personal communication the proportion of information conveyed by the actual words is less than 10% with non-verbal communication (in other words, body language) imparting the rest (Mehrabian's rule). Not only that, but if the speaker's words contradict what is being communicated through body language then it is the latter that will be believed. Body language includes tone of voice, speed and rhythm of speech, posture, facial expression and gestures. While you may query the accuracy of this proportion, nevertheless you should prepare to manage your non-verbal signals during an interview. Stating that you are completely confident in your project plan is less persuasive if you are, at the same time, protectively crossing your arms, not catching the listener's eye, speaking breathily and looking rather anxious. You should try to appear relaxed, perhaps putting your hands together rather than constantly fiddling with a pen, regularly making eye contact around the range of listeners and physically looking open, honest and confident, even if inside your stomach is churning with nerves.

Managing nervousness

Of course, panels do recognise that candidates are likely to be nervous because, after all, this should be an important occasion for them. Thus, it is wise, not just to give a good first impression but to recognise this importance by dressing in a professional way. Looking smart and business-like may also boost your self-confidence as long as your clothes are comfortable and require no fussing over. Information Box 9.1 provides some other guidelines to help you control your nerves.

Information Box 9.1

Guidelines for managing nervousness

- Make sure that you can defend every selection you have made in your proposal, from approach/paradigm to time-on-task for each component of your design, including why you rejected other possible choices, then you can be confident that you can answer most questions thrown at you.
- Plan your journey to the venue to arrive in plenty of time even if there are hold ups or transport cancellations. You can always have some refreshment in a near-by café and a gentle walk around the block reducing adrenalin levels if you are too early.

(Continued)

- Set out with a positive attitude because this is a great opportunity to meet and impress influential people, expanding your network and getting good practice in selling yourself, even if you do not succeed this time in winning the grant.
- Ensure that you have with you everything you might need such as: identification documents; your proposal and presentation if applicable (on a USB memory stick or computer and a paper version); a handkerchief; a pen and something to write notes on just in case; a bottle of water in case it is not supplied; a peppermint or two to freshen your breath if your mouth dries because of an adrenalin rush.
- If you meet with other candidates while waiting, resist comparing strengths and weaknesses. Chat with them in a friendly way about relatively superficial things rather than your proposed project. Ignore any attempts to undermine your confidence (not everyone has your professional integrity so they could deliberately regale you with their previous research successes).
- Pop to the toilet ten minutes before your interview time, do some shoulder shrugs to relax the muscles, take some deep breaths and paste on a gentle smile. Stretch yourself to be as tall and broad as possible – you will not only look more confident but feel more confident than if you slouch.
- Check the main marketable points of your proposal – know its USP (unique selling point) – and think about presenting them in a personable, confident way. That means not being arrogant or argumentative but being persuasive in a warm way when answering questions or giving a presentation.

Presentation

Unlike the question and answer session, a presentation is within your control as long as you have checked first how much time you are allowed and what resources, such as PowerPoint equipment and/or flipchart, are available or you can bring along. Preparation is crucial to ensure that you can make your key points in a clear, concise and compelling (the three Cs) way within the time allowed. Your slides should be tidy, logical and simple; often three key words or phrases per slide are enough as hooks to hang your ideas on, as aides-memoires and to keep the audience's attention. You should remember that a picture paints a thousand words, while diagrams and charts must be legible.

A presentation opportunity is not provided for you to reiterate your whole proposal but rather for you to elaborate on important aspects of it: the scientific value and potential impact of your research takes precedence over details of your methodology unless you are defending a radically different approach. Then you should marshall your arguments at a level suitable for your audience, avoiding jargon and acronyms. You may have been given a precise remit for your presentation, which you should stick to, or have been asked to address specific topics or questions from the panel. Make sure you do address these.

Try to begin by introducing yourself, using this opportunity to present succinctly your most salient skills, attributes and experience, chosen like your project topic to match the funder's priorities. Practise speaking in a measured way, using short sentences and pausing for breath, while looking at the audience, using eye contact. Practise again, and again, each time out loud rather than simply silently reading the slides because it takes longer to speak than to read. You should also practise looking at your audience while speaking rather than at a screen, which should only require a quick glance to keep you on track as you change slides. Then you should identify which of your slides you could skip over if you find yourself short of time. This is helpful to ensure that your main points are covered even if you are interrupted by questions or the projector breaks down or other nuisances that occur even for the best prepared researchers.

Questions and answers

You can do a lot in advance to prepare for the questioning section. For instance, you could identify colleagues who have had experience with your potential funder to check with them about the kinds of questions included and the tone and tenor of the interviews. Do they, for instance, tend to focus on some aspects, perhaps value for money or scientific merit, over others and do they tend towards an encouraging or challenging delivery of questions. You can check the funder's website to discern their priorities and main interests as well as revisiting the kinds of proposals funded previously (which you should have done earlier when preparing your proposal). Most importantly, you should arrange for at least one mock interview with a panel to give a variety of perspectives rather than with one individual, to practise answering a string of questions, although you have practised small groups or individual answers as advised earlier.

Remember that what the panel wants to know is whether your proposal is well thought through and likely to produce outputs and outcomes they need: basically, whether your objectives align with theirs and whether they are achievable within the time and budget available. Having previously taken every opportunity to share your proposal with peers who provided good feedback and likely questions that you can now readily respond to, you should also consider whether there are questions you are dreading. Those are the ones you should prepare for especially well, perhaps asking the mock interviewer to address that topic in some form.

We have provided some typical questions in Information Box 9.2 to give you an idea of the kinds of topics that could be covered.

Information Box 9.2

Some potential interview questions

- Why did you apply to us?
- What are the main aims of the project?
- What makes those aims unique?
- Please justify your choice of method/technique/sample size/ …
- Does your methodology have any special or unusual aspects?
- How will the budget be managed?
- Do you foresee any potential under/overspends?
- How timely is this work?
- What are the greatest risks to successful completion?
- How do you intend to cope with those risks should they emerge?
- What ethical/health and safety/legal issues pertain to this research?
- Who are the key experts in the field?
- How does your project align with their work?
- Tell us more about the potential impact of your results.
- Why are you the best person to lead this research?
- Where do you see yourself as a researcher in five or ten years' time?

It is best to consider a short response to each question but avoid trying to learn answers by heart because the gist may be the same but the format of the question – and hence your answer – may be different. You will also sound more natural if you formulate the precise wording on the spot. One sentence is usually enough if you follow it with a query such as 'Would you like me to expand on that?' You can have ideas for a longer version, with examples, at the ready in case they require more information. This should deter you from getting bogged down in long-winded explanations.

Should you find yourself, in contrast, with little to say in response, perhaps because you do not know the answer or do not understand the question, avoid waffle but instead be honest. Either say that it is a good question and you will make a (described) effort to find out the answer or seek clarification.

Sometimes, though, instead of asking a question the panel may ask you to give them an example from your experience of, for instance, a situation such as resolving a difficult situation or coping with unexpected challenge. In that case, you might use the STAR format.

STAR format

A STAR response should take about two minutes to convey and the acronym stands for:

Situation: provide the necessary background information concisely.

Task: describe what you needed to do.

Action: what you actually did and how, including the skills you displayed in so doing.

Result: detail the outcomes, emphasising the success point.

Such stories can be compelling if conveyed with enthusiasm and vivacity. They are used in many arenas to provide memorable information about things, in this case your prowess, in a subtly friendly but powerful way. Another powerful tool is to find an opportunity, if not already asked about it, to link your research to the funder's specific interests and reputation.

The value of this funding for success

One of the potential questions we noted was one about why you have applied to that funder. This is an opportunity to demonstrate that you are familiar with their work and strategic interests. It is also a chance to illustrate, in a genuine way that avoids being obsequious, how their support will be a recognised contribution to resolving an important issue. You might also mention how obtaining this funding would be a considerable help to you in developing your research portfolio and skills. They know that but will be glad that you recognise and value it, indicating a degree of humility.

One further request from the panel can be rather humbling unless you are prepared for it. It is to summarise, in lay person's language, the key points of your project.

Elevator pitch

Such a summary is sometimes called an elevator pitch in recognition that it is similar to responding to a question from a stranger in a lift/elevator within only a few floors to traverse. For this, you only have 20 to 30 seconds to introduce yourself, make a connection by saying what might interest them about your project and how it will be valuable to them. This is something you could practise for any kind of interview situation (also for some wondrous occasion, when your project is completed, when you meet the CEO of the company you really want to work for in an elevator!).

But that is jumping the gun somewhat. It is unlikely that you will be told immediately whether you have been successful. That result usually comes in a letter. However, immediately after the interview it is a good idea as preparation for future proposal writing and interviews to ask that you be sent feedback on your performance. It is also sensible to make a note of the questions that you remember being asked when you get home before they are lost in the business of life. In the following section we will explore the next stages of the process but first we illustrate some of the content of this section with Voice of Experience 9.1.

Voice of Experience 9.1

Reflections on interviews experienced

- Justifying the choice of research venue

What a stroke of luck! I was chatting with a colleague the night before the interview and he asked why I had decided to apply for a fellowship at XXXX University. To be honest, I hadn't given it a lot of thought other than it was close to home, I knew some of the people in the department from my undergrad days and their work was akin to my topic. It made me think about it more carefully and on the train to the interview I read up on their research record and preferred approaches to remind myself of what was appealing about them beyond the obvious and parochial. Good job I did; the second question from the panel was about the research context and I used the good rationale for my choice that I had concocted on the train.

Chemistry Lecturer

- Indicator of passion for the project

I have a sad tale to tell. On one occasion I had bounced into the interview full of enthusiasm, as advised by my mentor, declaring my passion for the project proposed. I thought I was going over well when one member of the panel asked me what I would do if I didn't get this funding. That was a facer! I replied that I would be devastated. Then he asked what my Plan B was. I didn't have one. After that I could feel the growing lack of interest as they politely asked some more questions but then brought the interview to a close. I clearly didn't get the funding and I can see now that they thought that my passion was short-lived if I had no back-up plan. Now I have a mantra derived from my favourite Scottish poet: remember contingencies – the best laid plans of mice (me) and men gang aft agley!

Professor of History

- Ability to deal with crises

I have had many salutary experiences related to interviews for research funding but the one that sticks in my mind was from a long time ago. I was asked to give a presentation so had prepared very carefully slides for over-head projection. On the day, the bulb blew in the projector and I was left without my comfort blanket. There was a flipchart, so I had to quickly and simply write on it the main points I wanted to make as I spoke. I could only remember the key bits and the writing slowed me down. Nevertheless, I got a round of applause at the end, and later the funding. I was told that the panel was impressed by my resilience, flexibility and concise presentation. It is fortuitous that they didn't see the over-full and tedious slides. After that, I was always succinct – and practised talking with and without my PowerPoint helper.

In conclusion, this chapter has reviewed the steps beyond the application form with a focus on the interview stage. In the next chapter we will move on to the steps beyond the offer of funding being made (or not).

Further reading

Aldridge, J. and Derrington, A. M. (2012) *The Research Funding Toolkit.* London: Sage

Berry, D. C. (2010) *Gaining Funding for Research: A Guide for Academics and Institutions.* New York: Open University Press/McGraw-Hill

Denicolo, P. and Becker, L. (2012) *Success in Research: Developing Research Proposals.* London: Sage

Punch, K. F. (2000) *Developing Effective Research Proposals.* London: Sage

10

First steps in a new grant

This chapter prepares you for:

- Accepting the award (or not)
- Getting your research started
- Moving on to the next thing

Introduction

Congratulations on getting your funding! It may come as a surprise (see Voice of Experience 10.1 for one perspective). You will only have a short time for celebrations, however, before you must move on to the task of running and managing your research project.

Voice of Experience 10.1

Getting the funding

What surprised me: That I actually won the funding. Applying for funding is such a mug's game, you get so excited by a project idea and work so hard on it and then it gets rejected. Every time you submit something you just expect it to come back as a no, yet you still allow a bit of yourself to get excited about it. When this one came back as a 'yes' I couldn't believe it.

Dr Marianne Coleman, University of Surrey

You will work closely with other teams across your institution but, as PI, you are the lead for the project and are, therefore, responsible for its smooth running. The steps involved can be summarised as follows:

- Accepting the award
- Activating the award
- Setting up the research project
- Monitoring the research project and final reports
- Getting the next grant.

In this chapter we will look at each step in turn.

Accepting the award (or not)

As the PI on the proposal you will need to officially say 'yes' to accepting the offered funding award alongside acceptance from a university administrator or other representative of your institution before the funds will be allocated. If you have been offered terms or finances that are not completely what you asked for in your proposal, then you will need to carefully consider the offer and be realistic about whether the project is still feasible and acceptable to you in its modified form. Negotiating the details may be an option. Occasionally funders, impressed with your application but short of funds or with a new priority in mind, may offer funding subject to certain conditions. These conditions may be what you would expect or come as a surprise that needs due consideration. For instance, they may offer less than you budgeted for in the hope that you can produce the same results, perhaps with financial help from others such as the institution in which you will be researching. It is important that you decide, perhaps after taking advice, whether you can produce the same standard of output as you would have with the original funding. It might be worth negotiating with them once you have marshalled your arguments. You could, for instance, suggest that some small aspects be omitted without detriment to the main project. Or your institution may be willing to provide more 'in kind' support if not additional funding.

Certainly, be careful about accepting a major reduction in funds just to secure a project for your CV; if you produce a poor outcome it will reflect on you badly. If there are issues that you need clarifying it might help to telephone for further information. If you think that there has been some misinterpretation of your plans that has led to required changes, then make your point more clearly in the revised version while responding to the specified points. Finally, remember that a prompt, polite response maintains your reputation as a researcher. This might be one of the scenarios where you decide *not* to accept an award.

Turning down an award may also occur if you are lucky enough to receive two funding offers on essentially the same proposed project. In such a case, you should talk with trusted colleagues and mentors about the best option for you and your future career. Also, depending on the specifics of your situation, you may also want to talk with the funders about any flexibility around start dates, your allocated time to certain projects, or partial funding. Your mentors and experienced colleagues will be able to offer advice and coaching for your specific case. Similarly, if on reflection you choose not to be funded by a particular sponsor due to changing personal circumstances, ethical issues being revealed about a sponsor that influences your decision, changes in world politics, or any other reason, then please talk with your mentors and those who have supported you in your application about your decision, and about if and how to decline the offer without gaining a poor reputation that precludes you submitting another bid at a later date.

If you choose to decline the offer then the next steps all become irrelevant in this instance, but if you choose to accept the award (which is most often the case) then alongside your acceptance, the university representative and others (such as the legal team) should carefully review the policies, terms and conditions of the award before the official acceptance is complete. You will be required to adhere to the terms of conditions of the funder, who will often put requirements on how you can report your research and on the way in which it is conducted. This might include specific ethical considerations or working practices. Unless you have already been through this process before at the institution where your project will be hosted then you will not know the specifics of how this works so make sure you are liaising with all the relevant teams including your institution's finance team to set up an account on the funder's grant management system.

Activate the award and get a funding code

You will then need to get to know your research finance team contact. Different institutions will have differing organisational structures in which these key people sit and will have differing names for the departments or teams; examples include: Research Office, Research Finance, and Research Services. Within the department, you may now deal with a post-award team member rather than the person who helped you with the budgeting, justification of resources and full economic cost (FEC) calculations at the stage of your application (pre-award). The post-award team member will help you set up your research funding codes and navigate the finance systems within your institution. These systems are not always straightforward or even comprehensible to the average researcher. Your finance contact will be invaluable at helping you navigate your finances including what is eligible for expenditure under different parts of your grant and whether or what can be vired from one section head to another. (To vire an expenditure means to move it from the code it is allocated to which may be overspent to another where resource remains – this is sometimes (frustratingly) not possible.) Indeed, research finances are another 'world' that we will not attempt to explore here other than the advice we provided in Chapter 6 on budgeting. The finance team members are the experts in this realm, hence the need to get to know quickly your research finance team contact.

Setting up the research project

This is the stage where, for many, the reality of the task ahead suddenly becomes starkly real and rather daunting. This often lets the Imposter Syndrome creep in again, oddly mixed with excitement and enthusiastic anticipation to get started, as our colleague describes in Voice of Experience 10.2.

Voice of Experience 10.2

The joys and terrors of gaining funding

First research grant – first, a feeling of relief that I would not be sacked (there is enormous pressure on academics to bring in money and this should not be underestimated). Next, a feeling of total panic that now I had to actually do the work!

The Fellowship (a few grants later) – massive relief for not having to teach for a while (too much pressure trying to do both and with kids). Excited about getting to work on something really interesting. Then complete imposter syndrome and a feeling of why on earth they allowed me to get away with getting the money to do something I wasn't qualified to do! Then (a few months later) realising that I can do it and actually starting to enjoy the challenge.

Dr Melanie Bailey, Senior Lecturer in Forensic Analysis and
EPSRC Fellow, Department of Chemistry, University of Surrey

The first thing is to acknowledge that the majority of researchers tackling the task of setting up and running their own research project for the first time find it challenging and demanding, conforming to the aphorism of being thrown into the deep-end to learn to swim. So, you are not alone. If you have moved to a new institution you will be also trying to navigate, quite literally, the unfamiliar territory alongside the inevitable new acronyms and unfamiliar systems and processes whilst simultaneously trying to establish the local network of people who can help you to do this. So, the second thing to acknowledge is that this stage will take time. Do not be panicked into trying to do too much, too soon, on your own.

The practicalities of getting a research project up and running will depend on several factors. If your research project is just you and your computer, with no ethical implications that would require consideration and approval through an ethics committee process, and no specific health and safety concerns, then getting started may be relatively straightforward. For many projects, though, this is not the situation. Here we will consider some of the things that you are likely to encounter when setting up your research project, with a focus on those who are moving into a PI role for the first time.

Ethics

All research has ethical implications but not all research needs to be reviewed and assessed through formal committees and panels to gain approval before you are allowed to proceed with your work. You will have had to consider the ethical aspects of your project in the application stage. Now, if you need to gain University Ethics Committee or NHS Research Ethics Committee approval or both for your work, you will need to seek out the appropriate channels and start the application process as soon as possible to minimise potential delays to the start of your work. Gain advice and guidance from the support teams at your institution on processes and timeframes. Often, the review process and any subsequent re-submissions can take a significant amount of time. However, you can progress other aspects while you wait for the relevant committees to meet.

Health and safety

As PI on the research project, you will be responsible for ensuring that the appropriate Health and Safety procedures and processes are followed in executing your project. Furthermore, acquiring your first research funding will often coincide with establishing your first research group and your first managerial responsibilities. Thus, you will then need to assume managerial responsibility for your team and oversee their safe working practices and conditions within your team. This may involve working in offices or labs within your institution and may also include team members who are doing field work or research activities outside of the institution.

Most research institutions have fabulous teams of people that will assist you in these responsibilities and ensure you have all the relevant information and resources to carry them out. Therefore, a meeting with the appropriate person from the Health and Safety team can usually be a great help. The 'Health' of 'Health and Safety' may also be interpreted as the effective managing of your team, including awareness and appropriate adjustments for disability, neurodiversity (that is, including dyslexia, dyspraxia, autism and other conditions), and mental health conditions. We will address this aspect, and considerations such as working hours, a little further on in the section that considers the Leadership and Management of a team, but first some more basic practical issues, such as procurement and networks of support.

Accessing or buying relevant equipment and establishing contacts

If your project involves laboratory work or using specialised software, computers or equipment then purchasing or arranging access to these will often be a major hurdle to overcome at the start of your project. You will have considered this hurdle as part of your proposal but the reality of buying and setting up new equipment can be another challenge to add to your growing list of initial challenges. Institutions will usually have a procurement team to help you with this, who will also be able to advise you about buying lab consumables and general ordering systems, as appropriate. Building your network of contacts *in situ* to include researchers from your department, technicians, administrators and the person (with varying job titles and roles from department to department) who is the go-to-person-for-any-random-queries is invaluable in helping you establish working practices and processes within your new environment and/or situational role. So, making time to join coffee breaks, seminars, and local meetings to meet people can all be useful on many levels. Another colleague reinforces these points in Voice of Experience 10.3.

Voice of Experience 10.3

Nurturing those who have special skills or access

In the olden days when I started as a lecturer, we had a central office for photocopying run by a Scary Dragon. Many of my colleagues tried their best to avoid having photocopies made, so sharp was her tongue. On listening to her a few times as I passed by overhearing unfortunate recipients of her tongue lashing who were hoping for a 'quick turn-around of materials' or 'some extras run off now' and so on, I realised that she

(Continued)

only wanted the respect she was due as a key person in the process. Thus, I made it my business to ask her what advance notice was required, how did she like the material prepared, was there a special form, etc. She gave me her rules and I studiously obeyed them, thanking her each time for her efficiency and taking a plant for her office team at Christmas. After a while, I too had an emergency request – and said that I realised that I was asking for exceptional treatment – but she agreed to it and I recognised how lucky we were to have her help in an emergency. I never experienced any dragon-like behaviour thereafter.

I think we all like to be recognised for our special efforts and don't mind going the extra mile when appreciated. Nowadays I make it my business to be thoughtful when dealing with any IT experts, official or a colleague in the same corridor, because I know they could do things with a moody computer when I may be in desperate need. Equally, I try to reciprocate by helping them in any way I can. It is called collegiality. It is what universities are supposed to be about, but sometimes are not.

An ancient professor

Recruiting team members and HR processes

If your bid involves staff members other than yourself, then creating a good team to carry out the work plans in your project is a hugely important task. If all the staff have been agreed and named in the project proposal, then you should work with your Human Resources (HR) team to establish their contracts. If the project also includes current institutional staff whose time will be bought out for the project, then you need to alert their line managers to the success of the bid (assuming that their permission to include this was obtained as you prepared the proposal) and negotiate the availability of this time. If you intend to employ new staff then you must liaise closely with your HR team because there are many regulations and laws related to employment that must be navigated and with which you must comply, wherever your national situation. Remember that this process of recruitment too may be time-consuming while the ideal person may have terms of notice to comply with, which again could delay the start of the project.

Many experienced researchers and academics will advise that getting the 'right' people to work with you on your research is crucial to the success of the project and that it is worth waiting and re-advertising rather than recruiting the 'wrong' person. All the recruitment processes such as creating job descriptions, person profiles, advertisements, arranging short-listing, interviews and the contractual details will usually be carried out through your institution's HR team in collaboration with you. Enrolling the help of an experienced colleague who has been through the same process is highly valuable for gaining insight into any 'unwritten rules' or local customs that may be tacit knowledge. It is helpful also to include a meeting between applicants and other team members who are already in place so that their views can be included in any selection process. They can also help pre-interview by determining with you the critical attributes required both for the project and to help the team work well together.

Leadership and management of a team

The role of the PI on a research project will vary depending on the project in question. In some cases, it will just be you doing the work as well as leading the work. In some instances, as a new PI you will be moving away from carrying out all the research work yourself to leading and managing others to do it. This can be challenging for many first-time PIs especially if you possess perfectionist tendencies. These perfectionist tendencies can be advantageous when meticulous data collection and analysis is required as part of your research, but then they make it difficult to trust someone else to do this work; those in this situation are often reluctant to let go of the work because they 'know it will be done properly' if they do it themselves or at least watch every step of someone else carrying out the task. The researcher who is new to management is often stereotyped as a 'micro-manager', that is, someone who is constantly checking every single element of what their team member is doing to ensure it is done perfectly.

A battle for perfection is but one aspect of moving from being a researcher to a researcher-manager. More generally, it should be acknowledged that just because you are a great researcher does not mean that you will automatically be a great manager (you may be able to draw on your own experience of being managed by researchers to validate this assertion). As a new manager, you will need to develop your management style, explore expectations, roles and responsibilities, and get used to delegating and being assertive. You are likely to need to develop an awareness of and appropriate adjustments for disability, neurodiversity (i.e. including dyslexia, dyspraxia, autism and so on) and mental health conditions to promote an inclusive and supportive working environment. (You can find an extensive chapter on developing inclusive environments in our sister book: *Supervising to Inspire Doctoral Researchers* which also includes a chapter on working with people from other cultures that may be useful to you as an embryonic manager.)

You will also need to consider the establishment of your group. Tuckman's stages of group development of forming, storming, norming and performing are worth considering and exploring because all new groups need to go through such a settling in process. Staff development or Researcher Development teams within your institution alongside mentors and senior colleagues will be able to provide training and advice to help you through this new territory. Nevertheless, be reassured that new people coming together to work as a team need to weigh each other up, test out boundaries and establish 'rules of engagement' or 'the way we do things round here' before they begin to work effectively together. Allow time (and patience) for these processes to unfold, remembering that you will be engaging in them too.

Be your own marketing department

A part of establishing your own line of research or your own research team is making sure everyone knows that you are the group that is 'working on X' or is 'looking at X in Y'. You might want to consider creating a Unique Selling Point (USP), for instance a short 'slogan' to describe your research direction. This is all part of raising the profile of your research and enhancing the appreciation and understanding of what your work is all about. This will in turn help with the dissemination of your work and to enhance your reputation, which will then enhance your chances of further funding. We provide in Information Box 10.1 a checklist of people who can be very useful in establishing and supporting your project.

Information Box 10.1

Checklist of people to meet when setting up your research project

1. Ethics advisors and/or approvers
2. Health and Safety advisor
3. Research Finance officer
4. HR representative – for recruiting team
5. Procurement team – for ordering new equipment or lab consumables
6. Mentor – to support and advise you
7. Line manager – to ensure a fit into the community
8. Facilities coordinator or similar – for space – and for desks/labs/computers
9. Departmental admin team – a fount of all knowledge
10. Graduate School/Doctoral College/Researcher Development team/staff development team
11. Disability/neurodiversity/wellbeing advisors for staff/students

Monitoring the research project and final reports

Depending on the source of your research funding, there are likely to be different requirements for reporting and monitoring progress with your research project. You may be required to submit interim written reports for the funder including financial information, outputs (including papers, presentations, public engagement activities) and other impact of your research. In the UK, many funders and institutions use researchfish®, which is a research impact assessment tool. Holders of UKRI awards are required to make an annual submission to this online repository so that UKRI can demonstrate the value and impact of the research they fund.

Some funders will have annual research meetings that you may be invited to or asked to present at. Maintaining a good relationship with your funder is important as there may be options to bid for extensions to funding that are open only to those who have current funding through their schemes. It is also likely that you will want to bid for other pots of money from the same funder and, in many cases, the reviewers and panel members will be part of the wider peer group of academics working in your discipline so will be part of the academic world in which you are navigating a course.

You will also probably have internal or institutional monitoring systems, which may be either formal or informal, for example, through probation targets, departmental research update presentations and mentoring schemes.

Once the project has ended, you will usually be required to provide a final overview of finances and expenditure, along with research outputs and impact. By keeping effective records and monitoring progress throughout the project, this becomes a simpler exercise to complete.

Getting the next grant

This is last on the list but should not be left until last! You will be looking for the next or complementary projects alongside running this project. This time, however, you will have the experience of having been through the process before and the knowledge that you can be successful. If you have maintained a relationship with your funder, this may help with securing further or extension funding from the same source. In all cases though, evidence of having been funded already and producing useful outputs from that funding will add to the 'business case' that you are a safe investment for research funding. If you are establishing a research group, you may also be mentoring your team to write their own bids and thus supporting the next generation of researchers.

As a final thought, please see one reflection on success in Voice of Experience 10.4.

Voice of Experience 10.4

Reflection on completion of a project

What I wish I'd known/someone had told me: I think the biggest thing is that if you are the sole researcher and principal investigator for your successfully funded project, it is an amazing achievement you should be damn proud of.

Further reading

For guidance on ethical standards and procedures, you could start with:

Standards and Operational Guidance for Ethics Review of Health-Related Research with Human Participants, from the World Health Organization (2011). Available at: www.who.int/ethics/research/en/

For guidance on health and safety in research, see:

Responsible Research www.iosh.co.uk/ushaguide from the Institute of Occupational Safety and Health.

For the stages of team development, see:

Abudi, Gina (2010) *The Five Stages of Team Development: A Case Study*. Available at: www.projectsmart.co.uk/the-five-stages-of-team-development-a-case-study.php
Tuckman, B. W. (1965) Developmental sequence in small groups. *Psychological Bulletin, 63*(6): 384–99.

11

Concluding remarks

Looking to the future of research is always tricky but we can predict that the Open Science agenda will continue to expand to enable open access to published research and to the associated data sets. The metrics associated with quantifying research outputs will also expand in parallel, which will be facilitated by new technologies. Keeping abreast of developments in these areas will put you, as a researcher, in an optimal position to reap the associated benefits rather than, for example, frantically catching up with any new rules on compliance. These developments, data sets, publications and metrics are outputs of research but first it needs to be funded.

Making predictions about funding can only be a best guess based on experience and such guesses are subject to the challenges inherent now in the super-complex world of higher education (Barnett, 2000), which in turn is subject to political, economic and environmental impacts. Our best guess is that it is highly likely that funding sources will continue to diversify and change, with the proportion of public funding generally decreasing globally but with funding from China, industrial and philanthropic sources becoming more prominent. Public funding will be more driven by societal challenges and policies that are designed to address global issues. Indeed, all funders whether governmental, charity, industry or other non-governmental organisations will probably become more directed by specific challenges or policies.

An example is the four Grand Challenges outlined in the policy paper by the UK government Department for Business, Energy and Industrial Strategy (BEIS). These challenges are: Artificial Intelligence and data; ageing society; clean growth; and future of mobility. This approach to funding research work tends to promote connections between fundamental academic research and technology/industry, and to encourage interdisciplinary/inter-sector working. Therefore, collaboration becomes an increasingly important component of the future world of research funding, especially international collaborations with China and with nations developing their research profile. This is manifested within the UK in the Global Challenges Research Fund (GCRF), where research forms part of the UK's Official Development Assistance (ODA) commitment, which is monitored by the Organization for Economic Cooperation and Development (OECD). Research must support the development in OECD's Development Assistance Committee list of countries and address some of the world's most challenging problems. For example, the call in 2019 was for bids on 'A Combined Food Systems Approach to Scaling-up Interventions to Address the Double Burden of Malnutrition' and encourages challenge-led and interdisciplinary research.

As engaging with end users and beneficiaries of research increases and the need to diversify research income grows, more research will be funded and commissioned by charities, philanthropic sources, non-government organisations and business. This kind of research is highly likely to not only be carried out in collaboration but will be co-produced and developed in partnership with academic researchers, rather than determined by the researcher exclusively. This will require a flexible approach and collaborative skills-set in future researchers (see book in this series entitled, *Inspiring Collaboration & Engagement*) as well as the ability to work with non-academic organisations and to engage with a diverse range of people. An example of the issues prevalent in inter- and trans-disciplinary and trans-sector research can be found in Antoine-Mousiaux et al. (2019) who discuss the framing of debates within the One Health community of researchers who seek to work across environmental and health science disciplines with policy-makers and citizens to promote human, animal and environmental health (see Further reading). We provide here an illustrative quotation from the abstract:

> Hence, to build such solutions, framing will have to be a conscious and repeated step in the process, acknowledging and explaining the diversity of viewpoints and values. The interdisciplinary dialogues inherent in this process promote translation between scientific domains, policy-makers and citizens, with a critical but pluralistic recourse to various framings of health risks and benefits associated with nature, and a deep awareness of their practical and ethical consequences.

There is a lot of advice available about achieving success in obtaining funding for your research. Our key piece of advice for the future of funding is that adaptability and flexibility are key skills to hone and future researchers should be prepared to meet the ambitions behind the calls as well as ensure they are flexible and able to adapt their research interests to the policy interests driving the calls. However, the main message that we would like you to take from this book is that, in order to navigate research funding confidently, you should not do it alone: this is not a solo voyage but one to be shared.

Further reading and resources

Antoine-Moussiaux, N., Janssens de Bisthoven, L., Leyens, S., Assmuth, T., Keune, H., Jakob, Z., Hugé, J. and Vanhove, M. P. M. (2019) The good, the bad and the ugly: Framing debates on nature in a One Health community. *Sustainability Science*, March 2019. Overview Article. https://doi.org/10.1007/s11625-019-00674-z

Barnett, R. (2000) *Realizing the University in an Age of Supercomplexity*. Buckingham: Society for Research into Higher Education/Open University Press

European funding opportunities: http://ec.europa.eu/research/era/index_en.htmhttps://ec.europa.eu/programmes/horizon2020/en/area/funding-researchers

Global Challenges Research Fund: www.ukri.org/research/global-challenges-research-fund/

Grand challenges: www.gov.uk/government/publications/industrial-strategy-the-grand-challenges/industrial-strategy-the-grand-challenges (updated December 2018 BEIS policy paper)

Open Science: further information and the agenda for open access to research publications can be found at the Open Science webpages: https://openscience.com/

Research Futures (February 2019) *Drivers and Scenarios for the Next Decade*. A study by Elsevier and Ipsos MORI. Available at: www.elsevier.com/ connect/elsevier-research-futures-report

APPENDIX A

Helpful websites for research funding

Where given, descriptions have been taken from or summarised from the websites

Raising funds in Europe

- Euraxess: **https://euraxess.ec.europa.eu/funding/search**

A pan-European initiative delivering information and support services to professional researchers. Backed by the European Union member states and associated countries, it supports researcher mobility and career development, while enhancing scientific collaboration between Europe and the world.

- European Foundation Centre: **http://www.efc.be/**

An international, not-for-profit association promoting and supporting the work of active European foundations.

- European Research Council (ERC): **https://erc.europa.eu/**

The ERC's mission is to encourage the highest quality research in Europe through competitive funding and to support investigator-driven frontier research across all fields, on the basis of scientific excellence.

- Funders Online: **http://www.fundersonline.org/**

A source of information on foundations and corporate funders active in Europe; also provides links to Europe's online philanthropic community. Remember to click on the 'translate' button if you do not speak German.

Raising funds in North America

- Big Online: **http://www.bigdatabase.com/**

A comprehensive source of fundraising information, opportunities and resources for charities and non-profits.

- Forum of Regional Associations of Grantmakers: **http://www.givingforum.org/**

A national philanthropic leader and a network of 32 regional associations of Grantmakers.

- Foundation Directory Online: **https://fconline.foundationcenter.org/**

Comprehensive database and search engine for grantmakers and the grants they've made.

- Foundation Search America: **http://www.foundationsearch.com/**

An online resource including more than 120,000 foundations and tools to locate grants by type, value, year, etc.

- Grantsearch: **http://www.aascu.org/**

A database designed for Grants Resource Center institutions (members of the American Association of State Colleges and Universities), and profiles more than 2,000 federal and private funding programmes that focus on higher education.

- Grantsgov: **https://www.grants.gov/**

Lists all funding opportunities from agencies of the United States government, e.g. the National Science Foundation, and the National Institutes of Health US (NIH),

- National Institutes of Health US: **https://grants.nih.gov/grants**

The largest public funder of biomedical science in the world.

Directories and books

- The Alternative Guide to Postgraduate Funding: **https://www.postgraduate-funding.com/gateway**

(Luke Blaxill and Shuzhi Zhou, Kings College London). Provides the tools and guidance needed to access charitable funding.

- Educational Grants Directory (Directory of Social Change): **https://www.dsc.org.uk/**

A comprehensive listing of national and local charities which give to individuals for education. Published every two years.

- Grants Register (Palgrave Macmillan) Hardcopy available through publishers (**https://www.palgrave.com**) or copies may be available in academic libraries.

The most comprehensive guide available to postgraduate grants and professional funding worldwide. A leading source for up-to-date information on the availability of, and eligibility for, postgraduate and professional awards. All information is updated annually.

Research councils in the UK for studentships and research grants

- Arts and Humanities Research Council (AHRC): **http://www.ahrc.ac.uk**
- Biotechnology and Biological Sciences Research Council (BBSRC): **http://www.bbsrc.ac.uk**
- Engineering and Physical Sciences Research Council (EPSRC): **http://www.epsrc.ac.uk**
- Economic and Social Research Council (ESRC): **http://www.esrc.ac.uk**
- Medical Research Council (MRC): **http://www.mrc.ac.uk**
- Natural Environment Research Council (NERC): **http://www.nerc.ac.uk**
- Science and Technology Facilities Council (STFC): **http://www.STFC.ac.uk**

Large academic charities offering full studentships

The Wellcome Trust: **http://www.wellcome.ac.uk/**

The Leverhulme Trust: **https://www.leverhulme.ac.uk/**

The Nuffield Foundation: **http://www.nuffieldfoundation.org/**

Carnegie Trust: **http://www.carnegie-trust.org/**

Student funding databases

Scholarship Search: **http://www.scholarship-search.org.uk/**

Postgraduate Studentships: **http://www.postgraduatestudentships.co.uk/**

Research and Development Funding: **https://rdfunding.co.uk/**

Research Professional: **https://www.researchprofessional.com/**

Student Cash Point: **http://www.studentcashpoint.co.uk/**

Charity search engines

* Charity Commission: **http://www.charity-commission.gov.uk**

Comprehensive information about every registered charity in England and Wales.

* Charity Choice: **http://www.charitychoice.co.uk/**

A comprehensive guide to charities in the UK.

* Charities Directory: **http://www.charitiesdirectory.com/**

Includes free list of charities, non-profit making organisations; message board, newsletter sponsors packages and charity articles.

* Funder Finder: **http://www.funderfinder.org.uk/**

This is a small UK charity producing online and offline applications, mainly for grant-seekers based in the UK. Some of the things they produce are free, some cost, though they may be available in libraries.

* Guidestar: **http://www.guidestar.org.uk/**

Has international partner sites, GuideStar International (**http://www.guide starinternational.org**) and GuideStar India (**www.guidestarindia.org**); features a user-friendly search engine to allow free and open access to information on all charities registered in England and Wales.

* Grants Online: **http://www.grantsonline.org.uk/**

This provides information, including email alerts, on funding from the European Union, UK government, lottery and grant making trusts.

* Turn2us: **http://www.turn2us.org.uk/**

This free, accessible website has been designed to help people find appropriate sources of financial support, quickly and easily, and has a huge list of potential funders, some of which are listed below to demonstrate the range.

* Aga Khan Foundation: **https://www.akdn.org/**

Grants made to students of excellent potential and track record. Usually made to support Masters study (although will consider PhD applicants) and made on a 50% grant 50% loan basis. Funds are also available to support travel and research expenses.

* The Ann Driver Trust: **http://www.anndrivertrust.co.uk/**

Grants for study of the arts, especially music – linked to particular institutions.

- Cancer Research UK: **http://www.cancerresearchuk.org/**

Offers a number of full PhD scholarships, in relation to cancer research.

- Carnegie Trust: **http://www.carnegie-trust.org/**

Carnegie Scholarships only available to graduates of a Scottish University who hold first class honours for research in any UK university.

- The Clothworkers' Charity for Education: **http://www.clothworkers. co.uk/**

Small to medium grants for postgraduate students under the age of 25 who live in or are studying in Greater London, or whose parents live in Greater London.

- Diabetes UK: **http://www.diabetes.org.uk/**

Offers a small number of full PhD scholarships for diabetes research.

- Leverhulme Trades Charities Trust: **http://www.leverhulme-trade.org.uk**

These awards are for those who can demonstrate a family link (i.e. parents or spouse) with the grocers' trade, chemists or pharmacists, or commercial travellers.

- Royal Geographical Society: **http://www.rgs.org/**

Awards for research expenses and travel for the study of Geography.

Glossary

Aim   The intent of the research, couched at a general level.

Audit record (finance)   The organised collection of invoices and receipts related to a project's costs.

Authenticity   The extent to which participants in interpretive research would recognise the resulting data as representing their world.

Bid   A research funding bid or research proposal is the application or business case provided to a sponsor or funder requesting resources to carry out the proposed work.

Calls   Themed or managed mode applications are when researchers are invited to submit applications within a specific area of the funder's remit. These may also be known as strategic or topic grants. Open calls are when any proposal within the full remit of the funder will be considered; these may also be referred to as responsive mode calls.

Case study   A research design focusing on one person, situation or organisation which traditionally involves in-depth study using a range of techniques or one or more techniques over a lengthy time period to produce detailed information.

Co-investigator (co-I) or co-applicant   A person who assists the Grant Holder in the management and leadership of a project.

Cost   The cost of a research proposal is how much conducting a research project will financially cost the host institution including all aspects, not just project specific costs. See also *Price* and *Full Economic Cost*.

Credibility   The degree to which participants would judge the research results to represent their perspectives in interpretive research.

Culture (Research)   The values and behaviours of a research community.

Data   Findings and results which, if meaningful, become information. In this text we use it to subsume all kinds of information derived from research activity, no matter the discipline.

Demand management processes Funders may limit the number of applications that may be submitted per institution by enforcing quotas, time restrictions or success thresholds. For example, funders may consider historical submission data to apply a success rate threshold that, if not met, will limit the number of applications permitted until the threshold is reached.

Design (research design) The structured approach to the collection of data that seeks to provide valid or authentic results using the most appropriate instruments in the most efficient and productive way.

Directly allocated costs The costs of resources used by a project that are shared with other activities. They are charged to the projects on the basis of estimates rather than actual costs. (These might be a share of the running costs of equipment or for goods bought in bulk for use across projects, for instance.)

Directly incurred costs Costs that are explicitly identifiable as arising from the conduct of the project. They are charged as the cash value actually spent and are supported by an audit record, i.e. invoices and receipts of transactions are available.

Environment (research) A term that is often used in funding applications to describe the resources, infrastructure, networking, mentoring and professional development opportunities provided by an institution and collaborators working on a research project.

Ethics The study of codes and principles of moral behaviour, and in research, decisions about which courses of action are morally right or wrong, particularly in terms of their impact on participants/subjects and the communities they belong to.

Evaluation An assessment or evaluation of worth of a phenomenon; the systematic collection of data about it.

Experiment A predominantly positivist research design in which variables are manipulated or controlled to observe the effect on other variables or in which research subjects are randomly assorted between experimental or control conditions and their results on a predetermined test observed.

Expression of interest (abbreviated to EOI in some instances) Sometimes called an 'intention to submit' application. A preliminary or first stage of an application process, usually a brief application process that is used for sifting applications with successful applicants being invited to submit a full application.

Full economic cost (FEC) A cost which, if recovered across an organisation's full programme, would recover the total cost (direct, indirect and total overhead) including an adequate recurring investment in the organisation's infrastructure.

Full economic costing A policy to support the UK government's requirements to improve the sustainability of research and other Higher Education activities by recovering as much as possible of the full costs from research sponsors, thus reducing the drain on resources supplied through central funding of universities.

Funders Sometimes called sponsors; those organisations, charities, businesses that provide the money to cover the costs of research projects. Funders may also provide other benefits such as mentoring schemes, networking opportunities and publicity for research work.

Gantt chart A visual representation of the stages of a project used in project management. Typically, a form of bar chart that represents the timeframes for different tasks associated with a project. A Gantt chart allows you to obtain an overview of dependency relationships between tasks within a project.

Grant Financial support for a proportion of the full economic cost of a project.

Grant Holder The person to whom the grant is assigned and who has responsibility for the intellectual leadership of the project and for the overall management of the research. In the case of a research grant this is the Principal Investigator (PI).

Grantsmanship The art, multiple skills, and craft of gaining research funding.

Grounded theory A research approach that begins by making no assumptions in advance based on literature/previous research. Theory is built up by induction using the analysed results of the empirical work.

Hypothesis A statement that should be capable of measurement about the relation between two or more variables. Testing hypotheses, and especially the null hypothesis, is part of inferential statistics.

IELTS™ The International English Language Testing System. An English-language proficiency test for non-native English speakers. A threshold score, which varies slightly between institutions, is required for acceptance on most doctoral programmes in the UK.

Impact (pathways to) Some funders require applicants to demonstrate how they will achieve the impact of their research, i.e. to explain the mechanisms of achieving the potential impact of your research.

Impact (research) The demonstrable impact that research makes to society and economic growth. Research funders have traditionally recognised three main types of research impact: academic, social and economic.

Impact statement Some funders require applicants to clearly explain what the potential impact of their research will be in a written impact statement.

Incubator(-like) companies Companies that help new and startup companies with training, space or other entrepreneurial support.

Indirect costs Non-specific costs charged across all projects based on estimates that are not otherwise included as Directly Allocated Costs. They include the costs of the Research Organisation's administration such as personnel, finance, library and some departmental services (such as IT).

Instrument A tool such as a questionnaire, survey or observation schedule used to gather data as part of a research project.

Introducing Members (IMs)   Usually two members of the funding panel or assessment committee who are assigned with reading your full application or bid. Full applications that need to be read and scored are shared amongst the committee, i.e. your application will only be read in full by the two introducing members of the committee; the remaining members of the committee will likely only read the title and the lay person summary, thus making these aspects very important parts of your written application.

Iterative design   An approach in which the results of one cycle in the process informs the next and the results of successive cycles are used to refine the ideas generated in earlier cycles.

Lay summary   A brief (usually a few hundred words) overview of the research proposal designed to explain the work to a non-technical audience who are not experts in that field.

Letters of support   Supporting documentation from collaborators or referees to enhance your application. Particularly important to illustrate agreement for use of equipment or resources on which your project is reliant for success.

Literature review   A critical evaluation of the most relevant documents (published and unpublished) on an issue in relation to a particular piece of research.

Methodology   The theoretical and philosophical case for the choice of research approach, design and techniques, including data analysis techniques as well as data collection tools.

Neo-positivist   Someone working with the philosophical assumption that the world exists outside the knower, that knowledge comes from collecting empirical observations and that we can develop coherent systems of knowledge (theories) through testing of hypotheses and logical deduction. There is a recognition, though, that all methods are imperfect, and that knowledge is inherently embedded within a paradigm and, therefore, relative rather than absolute. Nevertheless, it is possible, using empirical evidence, to distinguish more or less plausible claims, and to test and choose between different hypotheses.

Null hypothesis ($H0$)   A statement that no relationship exists between two variables. When the null hypothesis is rejected at a statistically significant level then it is considered that the hypothesised relationship does exist.

Objectives   Specific outputs sought by the implementation of the project that contribute to achieving the aim of the project.

Open Access (OA)   Free online access to research outputs. There are two main routes to making your research outputs open access: the green route and the gold route. In the green route, or self-archiving, authors make their final accepted (peer-reviewed) manuscript open access by depositing it in an open access repository. This route has no cost and usually the publisher retains the copyright. For the gold route, the publisher charges a cost for making the published version open access. This route uses a Creative Commons (CC) licence which sets the terms of re-use. The author usually retains full copyright.

Overheads Expenses incurred in running premises, such as building maintenance, heating, lighting and furnishing, and taxes, and/or in employing persons, such as employers' national insurance and pension contributions.

Panels The assessment and prioritisation committee for a funder, which scores and ranks applications to make decisions on the funding of projects. See also *Introducing Members*.

Paradigm A basic set of beliefs, values and assumptions that guide action and include the researcher's epistemological, ontological and methodological premises.

Participants Those people who take part in research of an interpretivist/constructivist nature and provide data for the research cf subjects.

Peer review Evaluation of the research proposal by experts in the same academic field.

Peer Review College The full list of reviewers and panel members, who are drawn from to peer-review and assess funding applications by some funders.

Population The totality of people, organisations, objects or occurrences from which a sample is drawn.

Principal Investigator (PI) The lead applicant on a grant or other funding application.

Price The amount of money that you are able to request from the funder to cover some or all of the costs of your research.

Pump-priming funds Also called seed-funding. Used to help researchers develop new and novel ideas that have the potential to be further developed in larger grants. Sometimes used for pilot data or proof of concept studies.

Qualitative methods Techniques by which qualitative data are collected and analyzed.

Quantitative methods The systematic and mathematical techniques used to collect and analyze quantitative data.

Reliability The degree to which an instrument will produce similar results regardless of who ever uses it or whenever it is used.

Research design A strategic, procedural plan for a research project, setting out the broad structures and features of the research, each with justification.

Research Organisation The organisation to which the grant is awarded and which takes responsibility for the management of the project and the accountability of funds provided. (That is why it is critically important to engage a Higher Education Institution's Research Finance Team in the bidding process – not only for the help they can provide but also to respect their accountability.)

Research question   A specific formulation of the objectives of the research project, often querying the general relationships between phenomena or the meanings attributed to them.

Sample   A subgroup of a population chosen for research when the total population is practically too large to study.

Seed funding   See Pump-priming funds.

Subjects   A term most frequently used in positivist research to describe those who participate in a research study of participants.

Survey   The collection of information from a sample of a population, using a questionnaire that might elicit both qualitative and quantitative date.

Tender   A formal process inviting suppliers or service providers to submit a bid to supply, for example, a piece of equipment. Usually several bids are needed in order to get a competitive price and demonstrate value for money.

Transferable skills   Those skills that can be used in multiple settings and moved from one professional environment to another, e.g. presentation skills.

Translational research   The process of taking basic research findings and using them in another setting, usually a clinical setting, i.e. using laboratory research findings to generate new treatments for disease; may be called bench-to-bedside.

Transparent Approach to Costing (TRAC)   An agreed methodology used by universities and other Higher Education bodies for calculating full economic costs.

Validity   The ability of an instrument to measure what it is designed to measure, that is the degree to which resultant data is appropriate, accurate and credible.

Index

www.ingramcontent.com/pod-product-compliance
Lightning Source LLC
Chambersburg PA
CBHW070932030426
42336CB00014BA/2635